MORE THAN PETTICOATS

REMARKABLE NEW JERSEY WOMEN

MORE THAN
PETTICOATS

———◦———

REMARKABLE
NEW JERSEY
WOMEN

Lynn Wenzel

Carol J. Binkowski

TWODOT®

GUILFORD, CONNECTICUT
HELENA, MONTANA
AN IMPRINT OF THE GLOBE PEQUOT PRESS

A · TWODOT® · BOOK

Copyright © 2003 by The Globe Pequot Press

TwoDot is a registered trademark of The Globe Pequot Press.

Cover photo: Courtesy of the Detroit Public Library, National Automotive History Collection.

Library of Congress Cataloging-in-Publication Data is available.

ISBN 0-7627-1272-4

Manufactured in the United States of America
First Edition/First Printing

For Jeff, the "wind beneath my wings."
—L. W.
For my mother and my father.
—C. J. B.

Contents

$\mathscr{A}$CKNOWLEDGMENTS

Our deepest appreciation to all who offered valuable research assistance, suggestions, and support to help make this book a reality. In particular we'd like to thank Bunny Kuiken at Botto House in Haledon; Ellie Kidd, historian at the Salem County Court House; the New Jersey Room, Alexander Library at Rutgers University; Bobst Library at New York University; the New Jersey Historical Society Library; the public relations office of Clara Maass Medical Center; the Ohio Historical Society; the Cumberland (Pennsylvania) County Historical Society; the Hunterdon County Historical Society; the Salem County Historical Society; the Metropolitan Opera Archives; the New York Public Library; the Oberlin (Ohio) College Archives; Howard University Archives; Princeton University Library, Department of Rare Books and Special Collections; the National Automotive History Collection at the Detroit (Michigan) Public Library; the library at Montclair Museum of Art; the New Jersey Division of the Newark (New Jersey) Public Library; and the public libraries in the New Jersey towns of Bloomfield, Montclair, Nutley, Hillsdale, and Hackensack.

Lynn would like to thank her children—Jennifer, Michael, and Stacey—for their love and support and her brother James and sister-in-law Francine for their encouragement and advocacy. She'd also like to thank her sister, Miae, who is a loving reminder of the importance of all the links, and her maternal grandmother, Grace Lillian Ziemer Hansen, for the stories she shared night after night about female ancestors—stories that inspired a passionate interest in the significance of women's roles in historical events. Lynn is especially grateful to The Thanks Be To Grandmother Winifred

Foundation for the generous research grant, enabling her to afford travel as well as to gain access to places that were gold mines of information. The book is richer for it.

Carol's special thanks go to her husband, Richard, for his support and continuing encouragement to pursue this and other worthwhile projects that have opened up so many new horizons; to her daughter, Daria, for her unique perspective and uplifting presence; and to many good friends who have generously shared positive input at just the right moment.

Grateful appreciation to our editor, Charlene Patterson at The Globe Pequot Press/TwoDot Books. Her superb editorial input and professional friendship are more than we could have asked for. Finally, thanks to Lynn Zelem for taking us across the finish line.

INTRODUCTION

As an original member of the thirteen colonies and the third state to become a part of the union, New Jersey's history is a long and rich one, and its women have made striking contributions from the first. Homemakers, farmworkers, slaves, aristocratic wives, domestics, industrial laborers, and even voters in Colonial times, they continually struggled for an equal voice and for educational and professional opportunities as well as to develop individual talents and create distinctive lives of their own choosing.

Thanks to feminist historians and women's studies professors, the field of history has grown to encompass the lives and deeds of more women than ever before. However, there is still a gross imbalance in the acknowledgment of women's accomplishments and, most especially, in the teaching of women's lives as nucleus of both history and society itself. History is still measured in battles and kings, in male genealogical family lines, and in machines and inventions for which the real inventors—often the wives of the men given credit—were lost in the darkness of cultural amnesia.

During recent decades, historians and teachers have begun to put women at the center of such great cultural movements as abolition, suffrage, temperance, religious uprisings and reformations, and civil rights and antiwar movements. A cursory reading of eighteenth-, nineteenth-, and twentieth-century social crusades reveals women as the framers of these currents as well as the foot soldiers who ensured that the battles for change were won.

Women were brave, innovative, steadfast, purposeful, persistent, and creative. They endured and exhibited enormous versatility and adaptability while striving to break through social, gender, racial, and economic barriers to improve their lot and enhance choices for their own and subsequent generations. The fruits of these struggles are tightly woven into our heritage, and those who affected these changes are finally being recognized. This volume celebrates the lives of a few such remarkable women.

Selecting a group of representative New Jersey women was no easy task. There are so many individuals with unique stories and important contributions to consider. Regrettably, there were many worthwhile women whose stories could not be included due to length considerations. They need another book!

The twelve women we chose, all born before 1900, came from different eras and varied backgrounds, lived in all parts of the state, and embraced many philosophies of life. Most of them are not well known, and we were thrilled to bring them into the light. Women such as Alice Paul and Mary Mapes Dodge, while familiar to some, had previously been presented one-dimensionally or only as footnotes in larger works. We are glad to present them here in more depth. Some women had to be omitted because there were simply not enough original records available. Perhaps someday dedicated historians will discover them and share their stories, too.

Women have been trailblazers in so many areas. We tried to present as broad a cross section as possible—from a warrior whose bravery helped save a battle, to a nurse who sacrificed her life so that countless others might live, to a labor activist who catalyzed a strike that ultimately changed labor laws, to a slave determined to live free and own her own land, to a fun-loving daredevil destined to be the first woman to drive across the country in that newfan-gled contraption called the automobile. They were all innovators—original, independent, and unique in their own right—unafraid to push beyond boundaries and defy convention. These women and countless others as yet undiscovered gave New Jersey a richness and character it would not otherwise have had.

An observer once commented that writer Mary Mapes Dodge embodied the "live spark of a woman." These women all possessed that spark—a spark that illuminated the road to great achievements during their lifetimes and, by their example, still lights the way for women of the contemporary world.

One further note: A study of history cannot help but present the researcher and writer with appalling instances of racism and xenophobia. Yet it would be impossible to uncover past mistakes without honestly acknowledging these historic flaws. It has often been said that those who do not study history are condemned to repeat it. With these twelve women and so many others like them as role models, may we, instead, go forward toward inclusion, enlightenment, knowledge, and justice. We hope that the women in these pages will come alive for each reader and inspire them as they pursue their own journeys to the future.

MARY LUDWIG HAYS MACAULEY

1754–1832

Hero of the Battle of Monmouth

*G*unshots and cannonfire exploded in the June air, already thick with the 100-degree blaze of summer heat and the putrid dust of battle. Molly Hays repeatedly swabbed, loaded, and thrust the rammer staff into the mouth of the cannon, readying cartridge after cartridge for fire against the advancing British forces. Despite steady enemy bombardment, and knowing that faulty loading could cause the cannon to explode, Molly continued unflinching, taking the place of her fallen husband, John. There was no one else left to load this cannon, so badly needed to be kept in action by George Washington's Continental Army and critical to the American Patriots' fight for freedom.

It was June 28, 1778, and the Battle of Monmouth was being fought beneath the wretched summer sun. Time and again soldiers dropped to the ground, as often from heat exhaustion as from their wounds. Some had merely fainted and were carried into what shade there was on the battlefield. But others perished from heatstroke, their tongues swollen and protruding. Some called out for mothers or wives; some mumbled incoherently in their delirium.

"The Heroine of Monmouth," Molly Pitcher

When Molly arrived at the battlefield, she was desperate to help in any way that she could. Grabbing the trusty pitcher she had used in the past to tend to those in need, she ran feverishly to a nearby spring, filling the pitcher and returning again and again. Over and over she lifted the pitcher to a soldier's lips, feeding him the cool water, giving him renewed energy for battle.

"Molly!" "Molly with the Pitcher!" "Molly Pitcher," cried the young men on the brink of collapse from the brutal heat. Molly rushed to their sides, dispensing water and scouring the landscape for the next soldier in need. She was gone before they could even gasp their thanks.

Molly stopped briefly to help a wounded soldier who might have died had she not hoisted him upon her strong back and carried him from the range of charging British forces. In a flash she was back to answer more fervent pleas for water. Although scores of soldiers died of heatstroke exacerbated by dehydration during the battle, many more would have fallen had it not been for Molly's help.

All the while, Molly's eyes frantically scanned the field for young John Hays. When she finally spotted and ran to him, he had just fallen to the ground next to his cannon. Although she poured water through his parched lips and bathed his head, she could not revive him from his wounds, or from the heat exhaustion that had overtaken him. Moving him to some nearby shade, she then stepped into his place—just in time to prevent his cannon from being pulled from use. Molly fought on until the battle ended at nightfall. This was one cannon that was not to be silenced in the quest for freedom.

Born Mary Ludwig on October 13, 1754, in Mercer County, a few miles from Trenton, Molly was raised in a German Protestant family. Her father, John George Ludwig, born Johann Georg Ludwig, had emigrated to the Colonies in September 1749 aboard the ship *Dragon* out of Rotterdam. After landing in Philadelphia he made his way to New Jersey, where he worked as a dairyman. Nothing is known of Molly's mother, but both she and her husband, immigrants from the German Palatinate, had emigrated to escape the triple burdens of oppressive taxation, religious persecution, and dearth of arable land and were ready to settle down and enjoy the freedom and bounty of their new country.

Christened Mary at the Church of Christ (now the Lawrenceville Presbyterian Church), Molly, as she was called for her lively personality, was a pleasing child and young woman with a ruddy complexion and a muscular, buxom figure. She willingly helped her parents with the backbreaking chores of farm life. As she grew, Molly heard much from her ardently patriotic family about the increasing tyranny of the British and carefully listened to accounts of unfair taxes and persecutions.

When Molly was fifteen she was asked by William and Anna Irvine, a prominent young doctor and his wife, to accompany them to Carlisle, Pennsylvania, to work as a domestic. Molly readily agreed. Mrs. Irvine was quite fond of Molly and treated her almost as a member of the family. Just down the street from the Irvine mansion was John Casper Hays's barber shop. The young barber and Molly fell in love, and on July 24, 1769, John and sixteen-year-old Molly were married in Carlisle. A notation in the pastor's records in the Church of Christ in Carlisle reads: "Married this day Mary Ludwig to John Hays. Mary is a simple kindly child of good faith."

After six years of quiet married life, John enlisted as a soldier in Proctor's First Pennsylvania Artillery, where he served as a gunner until his term of service expired in 1776. In 1777 he reenlisted in the Seventh Pennsylvania Regiment Continental Line, commanded by his young wife's employer, Colonel Irvine.

Feelings ran high in the Trenton/Carlisle/Philadelphia area against the British. The Tory armies had made quite a bit of headway against the Patriots and had defeated the Americans at Brandy-wine and Germantown. The long, hard winter at Valley Forge had bred despair in the ranks of the Continental Army. Still, the British occupation of Philadelphia, while discouraging, had not broken the spirits of the American army. Wanton destruction by bands of British marauders who had burned and pillaged homes and stolen livestock fanned the flames of outrage. When more than thirty women of Monmouth County were captured and raped, furious soldiers and their supporters channeled their hatred into a disci-plined fighting force, ready to take on the British army.

Carlisle itself had been a military post for many years and was an important point of rendezvous during the entire Revolutionary period. The road leading from Philadelphia to the western frontier ran through the town, and many thousands of Revolutionary sol-diers had marched through the little town, including General George Washington. Patriotic feelings engendered by these occur-rences stirred in Molly's breast as she went about her day-to-day tasks. And, of course, her heart was with both her husband and her employer as they marched off to war.

While the Continental Army suffered the torturously hard winter in Valley Forge, the British survived in comfort in Philadel-phia. They planned to depart for New York when the weather turned warmer. When Washington learned of these plans, he intended to intercept the British on the plains west of Freehold in Monmouth Country. This would be a prime location to win a vic-tory, since the Royal Navy would be nowhere nearby to support the British ground forces.

The early summer days were exceptionally humid and rainy during the late spring of 1778. Mud was everywhere, making the march difficult for both armies. British forces were further impeded by their supply train of more than 1,500 wagons. They hoped to cross New Jersey and reach Sandy Hook, where they would meet their navy and sail to New York. In keeping with his plan of intercepting the enemy while they were inland, Washington and his troops proceeded from Valley Forge on June 20 and reached Hopewell by June 24.

For a while after John left, Molly remained in the Irvines' employment. But one day a message came from her parents in Mercer County to come at once to see them. With that message came a letter from John begging her to make the trip so that they might have a brief rendezvous. With Anna Irvine's encouragement, Molly set off on the difficult 155-mile trip. She traveled on horseback the entire way, over rough roads and past occupation armies, her mind and heart eager for the reunion with her parents and some precious time with her husband. Finally, determined not to be parted from him again, Molly joined John, now an infantryman and a battery gunner, on the battlefield and in the military camp.

Molly's decision to become a military dependent was not an unusual one at that time. National defense during the eighteenth and nineteenth centuries was provided by volunteer citizen armies—often accompanied by their wives and children as they marched and fought. Although women's roles in these volunteer armies have been rendered almost invisible by historians, they actually played an integral and essential part in the day-to-day function of army life as nurses, suppliers, and fighters.

The army usually authorized three to six women per company to draw half-rations for themselves and their children in exchange for cooking, sewing, and laundering. But many others also joined their loved ones. Wives, widows, mothers, and daughters accompanied their male relatives either because they wanted to or because they had no other choice. Without access to military rations, they had to survive and feed their children by their wits and their skill. The women melted lead and made ammunition, tanned hides, spun linen and wool, wove cloth, sewed and knitted clothing, carried water, and tended the wounded and dying. They marched with the soldiers without respite, even when pregnant, giving birth, or nursing infants.

Influenza, food poisoning, and venereal disease were epidemic in camps and on battlefields. And there were horrible wounds caused by the slash of the saber, the tear of the musket ball. There was little that medical science of the time could do to cure illness or prevent wounds from becoming infected. "Doctors" were often untrained butchers who amputated mangled limbs without anesthesia and sewed wounds together with string, using the same needles over and over again without washing them—or their hands. Gunshot penetration wounds carried with them the dirt of the weapon, pieces of the victim's clothing, and splinters of bone. If the victim did not bleed to death, he ran the enormously high risk of dying anyway from rampant infection. Women worked to keep wounds clean, bathed patients until their fevers broke, spoon-fed broth to the injured, laundered bandages and fouled bedding, kept fires going in winter to warm the patients and, against all odds, tried to create a clean environment where men could heal amid the filth and chaos of war. And if a husband, father, or son fell to the enemy's fire, these women often took a fallen soldier's place on the battlefield.

Molly's contribution is, therefore, doubly important—not only because of what *she* did on the historic Monmouth battlefield but also because she represents the thousands of ordinary women who helped determine the outcome of the Revolutionary War (and other wars) through their courage, dedication, and skill in the face of unimaginable horror.

By June 26 the British had reached Monmouth Courthouse, and Sir Henry Clinton hoped to stop there and wait for cooler weather before proceeding to Sandy Hook. The Americans, however, were finalizing their strategic plans for battle. The strategy of the 15,000-strong Continental Army was to surprise the 10,000-strong British forces at dawn on June 28—first by attacking them from the rear and then by having additional forces attack at the front lines. However, General Charles Lee, worried that the Continental Army was no match for the well-trained and disciplined British forces, hesitated, losing the critical element of surprise. Then, believing he was outnumbered, he ordered a withdrawal of his troops. This not only caused confusion but also put the American army in severe jeopardy. When Washington learned of this, one contemporary said that he "swore 'til the leaves shook on the trees." Rallying the troops into the steamy sun, Washington ordered the attack to be resumed.

The Battle of Monmouth is said to have continued for twelve hours. Because the earlier advantage had been lost, the battle turned bloodier and more difficult. Long after sunrise, British and Patriot forces fought each other in the stultifying air. It was during this battle that Molly brought water to the beleaguered soldiers and took her husband's place on the battlefield when he fell. A Revolutionary soldier described Molly as "rather stout and red" at the time of the battle, "coarse and uncouth." Undoubtedly his description was correct. She had been functioning as nurse and warrior and must have been grimy with smoke and dust and smeared with blood. Like many of the soldiers themselves, she was also barefoot. Veteran soldier Joseph Plumb Martin later wrote in his memoirs that Molly looked with seeming unconcern as "a cannon shot from the enemy passed directly between her legs without doing any other damage than carrying away the lower part of her petticoat." It is also said of Molly that day that she rescued a wounded soldier named Dilwyn, who had been left for dead among those abandoned for burial, carried him from the battlefield, and nursed him into recovery. Molly's bravery and endurance at the Battle of Monmouth inspired her fellow soldiers to call her "Sergeant Molly" as well as to write of her:

Moll Pitcher she stood by her gun,
And rammed the charges home, sir,
And thus on Monmouth's bloody field,
A sergeant did become, sir.

This was to be one of the more controversial battles of 1778 and of the American Revolution. There were heavy losses on both sides, and the sun and the heat had taken a toll as significant as the gunfire. The British left their dead and wounded and fled to join the Royal Navy and sail for New York. General Lee was court-martialed for failing to attack as commanded, as well as for retreating and showing disrespect to General Washington. The outcome of the battle was indecisive, although Washington stressed the positive factors. After all, even though a real American victory eluded the Patriots, the British had been held.

John recovered from his wounds, and he and Molly returned to their quiet life in Carlisle, where their son, John Ludwig Hays, was born. Molly did housework and acted as a charwoman in the State House in Carlisle, and it is said that she specially scrubbed the courthouse steps on Independence Day and on the anniversary days of the Battle of Monmouth. John died a few years after the end of the war. Some years after his death, Molly married William Macauley (sometimes written McKolly, McAuley, or McCauley), a former soldier and comrade of John.

It was said of William that he "liked work so well he could lie down and sleep alongside it." Whether that contributed to Molly's dissatisfaction in the marriage we don't know, but she did leave him after a short time and for the rest of her life supported herself working as a laundress, cook, and nurse for the soldiers. She lived in the old United States Barracks in Carlisle, Pennsylvania, for many years. For a time she kept a small store in Carlisle and lived her later years in a stone house near the southeast corner of Bedford and North Streets there. Molly smoked a pipe, chewed tobacco, liked her ale, and swore like a trooper. Later in life she became stooped, her hair turned gray, and she became blind in her left eye where a particle of lime had lodged itself. Her daily outfit consisted of a blue-and-white skirt; a petticoat; a broad white cap with wide, flaring ruffles; a sunbonnet; wool stockings; and heavy, ankle-high work shoes.

Like many other veterans, Molly loved to tell tales of her exploits to all who would listen. Her son, John Ludwig Hays, said that his mother never tired of telling him the story of the Battle of Monmouth and her part in it. As she grew older, her tales grew more vivid. Her grandson related that Molly had told him that if it had not been for her, the Battle of Monmouth would have been lost. Her favorite audiences were groups of admiring girls. "You should have been with me at Monmouth and learned how to load a cannon," she would say. On patriotic holidays when local militia drilled, Molly would declare, "This is nothing but a flea-bite to what I have seen."

Molly's service to her country was never recognized by a pension, as was granted to other soldiers, but she did receive a lifetime annuity by Special Act Number 265 from the Pennsylvania Legislature on February 21, 1822, ten years before her death. The annuity was $40 immediately and $40 every six months thereafter. The *Philadelphia Chronicle* wrote of this: "It appeared satisfactory that this heroine had braved the hardships of the camp and dangers of the field with her husband who was a soldier of the Revolution, and the bill in her favor passed without a dissenting voice." Accounts of the time stressed that the annuity was given to her not because she was the *widow* of a soldier but because of her own personal services as a soldier of the Revolutionary War.

Molly died on January 22, 1832, of what was probably a bacterial infection from a skin lesion. She was buried in the Old

Graveyard in Carlisle in an unmarked grave. On July 4, 1876, the centennial year, the citizens of Carlisle had a stone inscribed and placed at her burial site, reading: "MOLLIE McCAULY Renowned in History as 'MOLLIE PITCHER' The Heroine of Monmouth, Died January 1832. Aged 78 years." A cannon rests by her grave, and atop it stands a statue of a woman with a cannon rammer in her hand.

Although other women performed acts of heroism during the American Revolution, Molly's contributions were unique. Her fame survives in the countless reminders that bear her name—a highway, a hotel, a 1995 musical by Barry Clay and, most fittingly, an annual award in her memory by the United States Field Artillery Association. Like many other soldiers, Molly covered up her kind heart and willingness to help anyone in need with a gruff exterior and brusque manner. She never had much schooling, and she certainly was not a learned person. But she deserves a special place in the annals of American history for her essential part in turning the tide of the British advance during the crucial Battle of Monmouth on that pivotal June day in 1778.

SYLVIA DUBOIS

CA. 1788–1889

Ambitious to Be Free

$\mathcal{S}$ylvia, a twenty-year-old slave, drew herself up to her full 5-foot-10-inch height. Dropping her slop bucket on the floor of the taproom, she raised her large fist, backed up by more than 200 pounds of muscle. After years of repeated whippings and beatings by her mistress with sticks, tongs, fire-shovels, knives, axes, hatchets, and fists, sheer hatred blinded her to consequences. Her cheek still bearing the latest imprint of her mistress's hand, Sylvia "struck her a hell of a blow" with her fist. The impact sent her mistress flying against a door and then onto the floor. Patrons of the barroom gathered around, thunderstruck at the sight of a slave striking her mistress. As they threatened to attack Sylvia, she raised her fists at them and dared them to wade in . . . and she'd "thrash every devil of 'em." Taking advantage of the onlookers' shock, Sylvia ran out of the tavern and, leaving her baby behind, set out north for Chenango Forks, New York, the first step on her way to freedom.

Sylvia Dubois, whose surname was that of her mother's second master, was born sometime in 1788 or 1789 at Rock Mills, Sourland Mountain, New Jersey, in a tavern owned by Richard

Sylvia Dubois with her daughter, Elizabeth Alexander, circa 1882

Compton, her mother's owner. "They didn't no more keep the date of a young nigger than they did of a calf or colt," said Sylvia in her reminiscences. "The young niggers were born in the fall or in the spring, in the summer or in the winter, in cabbage time or when cherries were ripe, when they were planting corn or when they were husking corn, and that's all the way they talked about a nigger's age."

Sylvia's mother, Dorcas Compton, was, as Sylvia said, "ambitious to be free." According to an unwritten law in New Jersey, if a slave thought a master too severe and the two did not get along, the slave had a right to hunt a new master. Dorcas was unhappy as slave to Richard Compton, for whom she did both domestic and farmwork, so she began searching for a new master. Borrowing money from a nearby prominent farmer, Dominicus Dubois, thereby indenturing herself to him, Dorcas bought her freedom from Richard Compton. But Dorcas was not able to pay Dubois back by the agreed-upon time and so became his property. Dubois, a New Jersey native born to a wealthy French family in 1756, was angry that Dorcas had not paid back the money she owed him; being stuck with the responsibility of Dorcas and her children further inflamed him. Consequently, he treated her very cruelly. When Dorcas's new baby was only three days old, Dorcas tried to hold a hog for Dubois while he yoked it. It was early March, the ground was wet and slippery, and Dorcas was unable to control the powerful animal. Enraged, Dubois whipped her with an ox-goad until she fell. The combination of exposure to the damp, cold weather, the whipping, and lack of childbirth care made her extremely ill with puerperal fever (a bacterial infection of the endometrium). She survived, but her recovery was long and arduous.

The lives of slaves were not easy ones, particularly in rural areas. The density of the slave population and the types of their living conditions differed widely throughout the state, depending upon the locale and the backgrounds of their owners. Slaves labored in the fields, planting, plowing, cutting, chopping, and husking. Women often performed domestic chores, as did Dorcas and Sylvia, although many doubled as farmworkers as the need arose. Some slaves were treated as distant family, their owners realizing that they were a valuable commodity and that good care ensured better work. Others were in poor health and poorly clothed, viewed only as living implements for ceaseless labor, and showed the permanent scars of brutal beatings.

Even if a slave had a reasonable master, this did not preclude some form of physical abuse. Runaways were common, and notices offering rewards for their return were seen frequently. Any slave who tried to escape, plotted a group attempt at freedom, or committed a crime against a master or his property was severely beaten or killed. Given the historically significant population of slaves in the state, it is no wonder that the Underground Railroad flourished in New Jersey by the early 1800s.

The American Revolution had done much to add confusion to the culture of slavery in the state. Some slaves ran away and joined armies on both sides. Others were sold at random to pay off the ever-increasing debts of war. In 1804, New Jersey passed an act to gradually free slaves. Nevertheless, this was not a complete grant of freedom. The young remained bound—females until age twenty-one and males until age twenty-five. And children could still be transferred as property. New Jersey had a handful of slaves even into the 1860s. Having known no other life, they were still being taken care of by their masters.

Once she recovered, Dorcas again went in search of a new master and freedom. She selected William Bard, who had sent food to Dorcas and her children when Dubois refused to feed them. Sylvia stayed with Dominicus Dubois when her mother moved on to her new master. Slave families were often separated in this way, with various members working in the households of different masters in diverse locales. Her heart heavy as she was forced to leave her toddler with Dubois, Dorcas mortgaged herself against a loan to pay Dubois for her freedom. Although Bard was kind, Dorcas still ached to be free and unsuccessfully attempted to buy her freedom. Shortly thereafter, Dorcas was sold to Miles Smith, a kind master. Still longing to be free, she again mortgaged herself to another family in order to buy her freedom from Smith. But Dorcas failed to make payment at the designated deadline and was taken back as a slave to Smith, with whom she spent the remainder of her days. Slavery was abolished in New Jersey in 1846, but Dorcas died around 1838. Despite her great efforts to be free, Dorcas died as she had lived, in slavery.

Sylvia's father was Cuffee Bard, a slave to John Bard. History records that Cuffee was a fifer for the Minutemen of Hunterdon County in the Battles of Trenton and Princeton during the Revolutionary War. It is not known whether he received his freedom because of his service, but he either did or could do nothing to extricate his wife and child from bondage. In fact, free people of color were constant victims of legal and customary discrimination.

Most slave women did not expect that their spouses would be able to protect them from violence and abuse. The rape of black women was a violent and dehumanizing experience for the victims and an emasculating one for black men, who, if they interfered, whether free or slave, could be beaten, killed, or sold. Separation was devastating and often permanent. White owners claimed that slave husbands and wives, despite "momentary distress," did not mind separations and "would quickly adjust to new mates." They also argued that "the separation of fathers from their children was of little consequence." History tells a different story. So while Sylvia's father fades from recorded history, it is quite possible he never faded from either her heart or that of her mother.

Sylvia remained a slave to Dominicus (whom she called Minical) Dubois and at the age of five moved with the Dubois family to their farm near the village of Flagtown in Hillsborough, Somerset County. No doubt she was performing household tasks even at that young age, as slave children were expected to begin working at around age six.

Slave children, through no fault of their mothers, entered the world with small chance of survival. Often fed irregularly and suffering from fevers, intestinal worms, measles, whooping cough, and other childhood diseases as well as tetanus and lockjaw, more than half never reached their ninth birthday. But Sylvia seems to have prospered. Strong from childhood, she flourished on dumplings made from cornmeal, meat soup, corn bread spread with a mixture of lard and molasses, apple pies, cider, and roasted potatoes.

Sylvia claims to have gotten along well with Dubois, in spite of occasional "severe floggings," but his second wife, Elizabeth, did not like Sylvia and abused her from the time she was about five. One day Elizabeth Dubois kicked Sylvia in the stomach so hard that her husband interfered, saying that Sylvia was too young to endure such treatment. At other times he told his wife that if she continued to beat Sylvia the way she had that she would kill the child.

Dubois's remonstrance only seemed to inflame his wife. On one occasion, when Sylvia admitted that she was "a little saucy," her mistress hit her in the head with a fire shovel and broke her skull, leaving a permanent 3-inch depression in the side of Sylvia's head. Another time, Sylvia's mistress whipped her around the head so severely that Sylvia bore the scars for the remainder of her life.

When Sylvia was fourteen she moved with Dubois and his family from Flagtown to Great Bend, his farm along the Susquehanna River in Pennsylvania. The Dubois family and their slaves traveled the 152 miles on foot and in wagons. Sylvia walked all the way, driving the family's two cows. After crossing the Delaware River at Easton, Pennsylvania, the travelers entered "a great forest."

The forest was then called the Beech Woods, and part of it is now the Pocono Mountains Recreational Area. It took them six days on foot to get through the deep woods full of wild animals.

When Sylvia moved to Great Bend it was still frontier, with only two log houses as a settlement. Dubois erected the first large frame house there, ran a successful tavern, and became a partner in the Great Bend and Cohecton Turnpike. The Dubois land was a central place frequented by travelers and where the trading of animal meat and skins often took place. Soon a village grew up with mills, homes, and storehouses. There were two boats to ferry travelers across the Susquehanna at Great Bend. One was owned by Dubois; the other, by a Captain Hatch. Sylvia ran the ferry and often stole paying passengers from Hatch by dint of speed and ingenuity. This pleased Dubois no end. She also operated a skiff, ferrying single passengers back and forth, for which she was well paid in shillings. Sylvia claimed that "in using the skiff, [she] could beat any man on the Susquehanna." Sylvia also made good money operating Dubois's ferry, an amazing accomplishment for a slave. Even then, Sylvia had already established herself as a singular woman in her world.

Along with hard work came fiddles and frolics. All-night parties showed Sylvia's skill as a dancer. She stated proudly that when she was young, she could "cross my feet ninety-nine times in a minute and never miss the time, strike heel or toe with equal ease, and go through the figures as nimble as a witch." There was also peach and apple brandy, rum and holiday celebrations at Easter, Christmas, New Year's Day, and the Fourth of July. But Sylvia was still a slave and subject to the whims of her mistress and occasional floggings from her master. As Sylvia explained it, masters would give their slaves a holiday to have a little sport, then, if the slaves had any fun (drinking, making noise, celebrating), their owners would tie them to a post, flog them on their bare backs until they were nothing but slits, gashes, and strings of flesh, and then wash the wounds in salt.

By 1808 Sylvia had grown into a large, strong young woman with a powerful reserve of resentment and hatred toward her mistress. And she had vowed that when she grew up she would pay her mistress back. And so she did, striking her mistress a mighty blow, knocking her down, leaving her babe behind, and running away to Chenango Forks across the state line in New York, where she went to work.

Dominicus Dubois was not at home during this fateful time. Sylvia often said that the incident might not have happened had he been there to protect her and diffuse the situation. But when he returned home after serving on the grand jury at Wilkes-Barre, he sent for Sylvia to come back. When asked why she returned, she replied, "I was a slave, and if I didn't go, he would have brought me, and in a hurry too; in those days, the master made the niggers mind; and when he spoke, I knew I must obey. . . . Them old masters, when they got mad, had no mercy on a nigger—they'd cut a nigger all up in a hurry—cut 'em all up into strings, just leave the life, that's all; I've seen 'em do it, many a time."

But when Sylvia returned, she was not "scolded" much. Seeing that Sylvia and his wife would never get along, and being fond of his young, hardworking, resourceful slave, Dubois told Sylvia that if she would take her child and go to New Jersey and stay there, he would give her her freedom. Late that night, Dubois wrote her a pass, and early the next morning Sylvia set out for Flagtown a free woman.

On foot and carrying Moses, her year-and-a-half-old baby, Sylvia began the long 152-mile trek back to Flagtown. Day and night she walked through the thick Beech Woods, a place so deserted there were days when she didn't see another human being. Drawing on reserves of strength, without enough food, sleeping on a bed of leaves and pine needles when she was too tired to go on, Sylvia made her way back home. The woods were full of panthers, bears, wildcats, and wolves. Sylvia often spotted them during the day and at night their howls "made the hair stand up all over [her] head."

One day as Sylvia walked toward Flagtown, a man called to her, asking, "Whose nigger are you?" This was a frightening moment because, in those days, blacks were not allowed to go any-where without a pass. Anyone could stop a Negro traveler and demand to know whom he or she belonged to; a Negro who did not show a pass or did not have one was arrested at once and con-fined until retrieved by his or her master.

Again, the powerful and courageous Sylvia spoke up for her-self and her child. "I'm no man's nigger—I belong to God—I belong to no man." The man then asked, "Where are you going?" And Sylvia replied, "That's none of your business—I'm free; I go where I please."

When the man came threateningly toward Sylvia, she calmly set her baby down on the ground, raised her fist, and stared at him. He backed off, but not without the threat to have her arrested as soon as he found a magistrate.

At Easton, Pennsylvania, strangers helped Sylvia cross the Delaware aboard a raft. There was just one goal in Sylvia's mind—to find her mother. Upon arriving in Flagtown, she discovered that her mother had moved to New Brunswick as slave to Miles Smith. Dorcas and Sylvia were reunited, and Sylvia remained with her mother for several years, working and raising her child.

This period allowed Sylvia to achieve a change in status, from freed slave to wage earner, but her life became little easier because of it. Due to extremely limited education and employment oppor-tunities, few free women of color were able to reach or maintain a comfortable lifestyle. Most found work as washerwomen, maids, cooks, day laborers, or seamstresses, and their social and economic status remained low in every respect. Only in miniscule numbers were free women of color able to own a business or land.

Sometime around 1811 Sylvia found permanent work with the Louis Tulane family in Princeton. Sylvia spoke fondly of the entire family, referring to son Victor as "a great man, a good man," and Madam Tulane as "a good woman." No doubt working as a house servant, Sylvia remained in the employ of the Tulanes for fifteen to twenty years.

Around 1830, Sylvia's maternal grandfather, manumitted slave Harry Compton, asked her to return to Sourland Mountain to care for him during his final illness and run his tavern at Rock Mills. At this time Harry Compton was reputed to be more than a hundred years old. He, too, had been "ambitious to be free" and had managed to buy his freedom from his master, Richard Compton, by owning and running charcoal pits, accumulating enough money not only to buy his freedom but also to purchase land and build a house. Sylvia stayed with her grandfather until he died, sometime before 1840. At his death Sylvia became the exception to the rule for free people of color—she inherited Compton's land and property at Cedar Mills, the most elevated portion of the Sourland Mountain.

The large tavern that Sylvia inherited had a rich history. Standing along the road that extended westward from Rock Mills near its intersection with the road that runs from Wertsville to Hopewell, it was called Put's Tavern after Harry Compton's first owner, General Rufus Putnam, whom Harry thought more distinguished than either of his other two owners and whose name he preferred to use. When Harry became proprietor of a hotel and a man of note as a tavern keeper, his patrons began calling him Harry Put, and the name stuck.

Put's Tavern, though never licensed, was famed far and near for its sporting characters, race mixing, cockfights, fox chases, prizefights, gambling, and fancy women. The hotel was large, consisting of four rooms on the first floor and a story above also divided into rooms. It had a porch with many windows and doors, which stretched the entire length of the front. The whole was surrounded by virgin forest that extended for miles in every direction. Drawn by the freedom to gamble and couple at will, guests came from far and wide to experience Harry Compton's hospitality—from Trenton and Princeton, from New Brunswick, New York, and Philadelphia. Such was the enterprise that Sylvia inherited.

It was common practice for wives and widows to keep taverns as a means of livelihood, especially in the New England and Mid-Atlantic states, and Sylvia ran Put's Tavern for several years. But as the years went by, as clientele dwindled and the forest surrounding the tavern was sold for lumber, as land was tilled and "civilization" encroached upon the old place, it fell into disrepute. People "legally" trying to steal her property out from under her constantly aggrieved Sylvia. In 1840 Put's Tavern was burned to the ground while Sylvia was away. She lost everything, including furniture, books, and cooking utensils. Many of the items, including a family Bible, were stolen before the building was burned and were later found scattered over the mountain.

Sylvia always blamed "the damned Democrats" (at that time, the party of slavery) for setting fire to her house, but no one was ever arrested or brought to justice for the deed. No lawyer would take Sylvia's case because she had no money. Undaunted, Sylvia persevered. She still had her freedom and her land. She rebuilt a house of cedar poles and brush made in the style of a wigwam where she lived alone (except for the companionship of her pet sow and chickens) and supported herself by breeding prize hogs for almost thirty years. In fact, Sylvia's hogs were so highly regarded that farmers would often come a long way to purchase a prime animal from Sylvia's herd. In the 1870s "them damned Democrats" burned Sylvia's mountain home again, and this time—aged, penniless, and disheartened—she went to live with her next-to-youngest daughter, Elizabeth Alexander, called "Lizi," the only one of her six children still living. (History does not reveal what happened to the rest of her children—Moses, the baby she carried to freedom, Judith, Charlotte, Dorcas, and Rachel, born in 1827.) Elizabeth's home near Ringoes in Hunterdon County was at one of the highest points of Sourland Mountain, with beautifully rugged terrain and an impressive view. The cabin, a 10-foot-square log hut, was simple and rustically furnished, yet it was practical and hospitable. Elizabeth, who took after her mother in size and pugilistic ability, was a champion amateur boxer as well as a fortune-teller.

Sylvia lived with Elizabeth, who had been born in 1824, for almost twenty years and died in Elizabeth's rural home on May 1, 1889. Her will, proved in Flemington on May 7, named her "beloved daughter Elizabeth" as sole inheritor of all Sylvia's personal and real estate. Sylvia was one hundred years old, having outlived her master, Dominicus Dubois, by more than sixty-five years and her cruel mistress by more than forty.

Sylvia Dubois was a woman of unrestrained passions. "Bondage, or even restraint, [was] near akin to death for Sylvia." Her desire to be free in all things—speech, work, and appetites—was her life's goal. To attain and keep this goal, she chose to live in the poorest possible way in the most primitive areas, with little of material value or sustenance. She spurned her culture's tyrannies of decorum and femininity and played neither the docile slave nor the passive woman. Sylvia not only bested men physically but also was able to survive economically in a masculine world earning a living by the sweat of her brow. In her mind, she was the wealthiest of women, for she was dependant on no one and died as she had lived—free in heart, mind, spirit, and body.

Authors' note: In 1883 Sylvia Dubois was interviewed by Cornelius Wilson Larison, a physician and founder of the Academy of Science and Art at Ringoes, New Jersey. Larison practiced medicine in Somerset and Hunterdon Counties and became acquainted with many of the residents there. He enjoyed delving into local history and felt that many of his aging patients had important stories to tell that would illuminate the local past. Sylvia was unique. She was reported to be well over one hundred years old (later disproved) and had witnessed important history firsthand. Larison was compelled to meet this remarkable woman and transcribe her story before it was lost.

Larison interviewed Sylvia early in 1883, recording her reminiscences and adding his own commentary. The interview was printed later that year. A facsimile reprint was issued in the 1960s by the Negro Universities Press, and it was somewhat difficult reading because of Larison's innovative phonetic spelling style. The text was transcribed, edited, and reissued twenty years later as part of the thirty-volume Schomburg Library of Nineteenth-Century Black Women Writers so that the life of this remarkable woman could be available to a wider readership.

We can be certain that Larison, a white male in a patriarchal world, censored some of Sylvia's words and superimposed his own nineteenth-century prejudices on her voice. We also know that Sylvia withheld information on her husband and the conception of her children from Larison. Yet his contribution cannot be denied. Larison gives us a unique look at a woman who endured the trials of slavery, gained her freedom, took an independent stand, and persevered through many hardships. Sylvia said to Larison, "If you think what I tell you is worth publishing, I will be glad if you do it. T'won't do me no good, but maybe t'will somebody else."

ABIGAIL GOODWIN
1793–1867

Champion of the Underground Railroad

*A*ll day snow had threatened, and now, in the dark of night, it fell heavily. Abigail had hung a lantern outside her home to let escaping slaves know that here was a "safe house" where they could find respite. Still, she waited fearfully. Anxiously she opened and closed the door many times, hoping that the struggling band of escapees would be able to see the lantern through the heavily falling snow, that they would be able to make their way on foot through the deep drifts without being discovered by slave catchers. Fortunately the heavy snow blanketed sound—but it also froze bare feet and fingers. Finally, sometime in the middle of the night, the struggling slaves arrived. They were very thin, and they shivered with cold that the few rags they wore could not keep out. Two of the children were ill with fever. One of the women had a terrible cough. Another had an infected foot that caused her great pain. It seemed impossible to believe that the little forty-seven-year-old woman ushering them into her cozy house could be their savior. Yet it was true. Abigail closed and bolted the door. She sat the weary slaves down in front of a crackling fire, wrapped them in blankets, and gave them food to eat. Later that night she would find them all a warm place to sleep until they could start once again on the Underground Railroad to freedom. After all, her stop was but one in a long line of secret "stations." But for tonight, at least, the auction block, the whip, and the bloodhounds seemed far away. Thanks to Abigail, this night they were safe.

Abigail Goodwin was born on December 1, 1793, in the town of Salem in Salem County, New Jersey. She was the fifth of six daughters born to farmers William Goodwin and Elizabeth Woodnutt Goodwin. Both Goodwins had a long history in New Jersey going back to the late 1600s when the first Woodnutt came from England and settled in Salem, where he was an original member of the Society of Friends and built the Quaker meetinghouse. Salem itself first began as the Fenwick Colony of Friends at Elsinborough Point, later named New Salem on August 26, 1675. Both Abigail's father and her uncle, following the practice of most Quakers of Salem County, had freed their slaves during the American Revolution.

Although little has been written about Abigail from her birth until 1814, it is known that she grew up embracing the traditions of the Religious Society of Friends. Evidently she received some formal education through the Society's school, because she demonstrated literary and mathematical fluency in later years.

Minutes from the Female Benevolent Society of Salem indicate that Abigail was among the founders of this group in 1814 and that she was part of their Committee to Visit the Sick for a number of years. The Society served as a relief organization that helped widows as well as the ill, aged, and unemployed. She led a busy life with this charitable work and for fifty-three years never ceased her efforts on behalf of the Society.

But for a woman whose life deeply affected so many others

and whose bravery saved so many lives, her own life was obscure. From the age of forty-four until she died at seventy-four, she worked tirelessly as an active abolitionist and engaged in correspondence with many leading thinkers and abolitionists, yet history rarely remembers her name. In this way Abigail lived her Quakerism, allowing the light of goodness to shine *through* her rather than *on* her. She embodied the Biblical injunction to "do unto others as you would have others do unto you," saying, "Inasmuch as ye have *not* done it unto one of the least of these my brethren, ye have *not* done it unto me."

One cannot separate Abigail's work from her Quaker beliefs, for it was never enough for Quakers to *have* beliefs; it also was incumbent upon them to *live* them. Quakers believe that divine revelation is immediate and individual, that all individuals may perceive the word of God in their soul, terming this revelation the "inner light." They rejected paid clergy set apart from the rest and emphasized human goodness, believing that something of God exists in everyone. Truth and sincerity were essential. Quaker boys and girls were taught to be gentle, moral, and loving and to reject the trappings of the material world. Charity to the poor and less fortunate was an essential part of life.

Quakers were often the driving force behind nineteenth-century reform movements, not only on slavery but also on temperance, peace, asylums, penitentiaries, education, and Native American rights. Later, the nineteenth-century women's movement and the push for equal suffrage grew directly out of these earlier reform crusades. Quakers became active in abolition during the 1750s, first freeing their own slaves and then working to persuade other Americans of the need to abolish slavery. After the Revolution they created manumission societies, defended the rights of free people of color, aided runaway slaves, and lobbied state and federal governments to end the slave trade and eliminate slavery.

How could they do otherwise, they argued, when their religion taught them that all people were innately equal? How could they not live the Biblical injunction from Hebrews 13:3 to "Remember them that are in bonds as bound with them."

Quiet Abigail was a reader and a great correspondent. As a young girl she no doubt read the book *Mental Improvement* by Priscilla Wakefield, which contained stories about the slave trade, the capture of blacks on the Guinea coast, the separation of families, and the packing of the slaves into the holds of slave ships. She would have read that most of the slaves died from lack of air, water, and food, while others threw themselves into the sea or were maimed by cruel shipmasters. She probably also read Thomas Clarkson's *An Essay On Slavery*, wherein the horrors of slavery—the torture of defiant slaves, the rape of women, and the murder of slaves for insurance money—were outlined. Abigail's friend Lucretia Mott had read both as a young girl, and they had formed her position on slavery thereafter. Through letters and their occasional visits to Salem, Abigail became friends with such abolitionists and feminists as Harriet Forten Purvis, Alba Alcott, Angelina and Sarah Grimke, Abby Kelley Foster, and Lydia Maria Childs. Perhaps most important, she became a correspondent with and friend of abolitionist and founder of the Philadelphia Female Anti-Slavery Society, Ester Moore, as well as Presbyterian Minister James Miller McKim and Philadelphia Underground Railroad "stationmaster" William Still.

Abigail may have been quiet and plain, but she was vociferous in her advocacy of the slaves' cause. A friend of Abigail's wrote, "You may wonder why her sister, E [Abigail's sister Elizabeth] . . . seems to be so much less known among antislavery people than Abbie? One reason is that although dear Betsy's interest in the subject was quite equal in *earnestness,* it was not quite so absorbingly *exclusive.* . . . Abby denied herself even *necessary* apparel, and Betsy has often said that few beggars came to our doors whose garments were so worn, forlorn, and patched-up as Abby's. Giving to the colored people was a perfect *passion* with her."

New Jersey's slave traditions had a diverse history, and practices varied greatly within the state. East Jersey was originally dominated by planters who needed significant numbers of slaves to work on large tracts of land. In comparison with the milder Dutch attitudes, these owners treated slaves harshly, replicating practices from their native Barbados. West Jersey was inhabited by a large number of Quakers. Although there was some slavery within this area, it was minimal, and these slaves were usually treated less harshly. Eventually Queen Anne united East and West (now South) Jersey into one royal colony and encouraged the Royal African Company to bring increasing numbers of slaves to its shores. By the early 1700s Perth Amboy was a major slave center and holding area.

During the American Revolution, some slaves ran away and joined armies on both sides. Others were sold to pay off ever-increasing war-related debts. Although Quakers were not primarily slave owners, those who did have slaves freed them during the Revolutionary War. Despite the fact that New Jersey continued to table antislavery legislation, the Quakers passed a decree of their own that no one from the Society of Friends was permitted to have slaves. John Cooper of Gloucester summed up the Quaker stand on slavery when he said that the public, while fighting for their own liberty, should contemplate "our fellow men who are now groaning in bondage under us."

Ultimately New Jersey passed an ordinance in 1804 to free slaves gradually. But this was a halfway measure. Young females were held bound until age twenty-one, males until age twenty-five. Children could still be transferred as property. Ironically, although New Jersey had been a colony and state whose citizens had spoken out on behalf of freedom, it was the last of the Northern states to still have slaves, even after the Civil War.

Abigail's work was part of an essential network that received, hid, clothed, fed, and sent fugitive slaves North and, eventually, to Canada. The entire area of South Jersey—from Cape May to Greenwich and including Salem—was a favorite destination for runaway slaves from Delaware, Maryland, and Washington, D.C., and the Goodwin site was a critically important one. No one knows exactly how many fleeing slaves used this Underground Railroad. It was dangerous to keep records, and after the Fugitive Slave Act of 1850, which called for large fines and prison terms for those aiding runaway slaves, most existing records were destroyed. But it has been estimated that as many as 50,000 souls may have used the different branches of the Railroad in New Jersey. And it is known that one of the most widely used stations was the one conducted by Abigail with the help of her sister, Elizabeth, in order to "overthrow the demon, Slavery."

In 1837, at the request of Quaker abolitionist Mary Grew, Abigail took on the superintendence of Salem County, although she wrote that while she was truly willing, she feared her list of prospective supporters would not be a long one. For the remainder of her life, she worked ceaselessly to raise money for fleeing slaves and offered her home as an essential stop on the Railroad. Her heart particularly went out to slave children, of whom she wrote, "Slavery is particularly hard for children, that cannot do anything to protect themselves, nor can their parents, and the old, too; it is hard for them. . . . Will that little boy of seven years have to travel on foot to Canada? There will be no safety for him here."

In the course of their abolitionist work, Abigail and Elizabeth often sheltered controversial figures. Daniel Drayton, a Quaker abolitionist who had served a four-year prison sentence for transporting seventy-five runaway slaves aboard his ship, was a guest at the Goodwin home. In spite of his pardon by President Millard Fillmore, he was the target of virulent antiabolitionist sentiment in the area.

Another incident occurred around the visit of James Miller McKim, who had been invited by Abigail to lecture to a group of Quaker women who wanted to help runaway slaves. During his first lecture, a drunken man interrupted and before he could be subdued, a noisy throng of men and boys rushed into the room, ending the lecture and forcing McKim and his audience to leave the courthouse. The mob followed them, hurling threats of tar and feathers, blasting horns, and banging on tin kettles. Undeterred, McKim and the Quaker women scheduled a second lecture. It never took place. A mob of antiabolitionists assembled once more and paraded through the streets of Salem with an effigy of McKim, setting it on fire in the center of town. Around midnight the vicious mob attacked Abigail's house with clubs, beating at doors and windows and shouting for "that d——d abolitionist" to come out.

A local newspaper, the *Freeman's Banner,* reported these incidents in disbelief: "We did not suppose that our heretofore peaceable town contained the material to raise a mob and create a riot. But we were sorrowfully disappointed." None of these frightening events deterred Abigail.

In her concern for slaves, Abigail did not fail to link all oppressed people together. She was particularly aware of how the roles women were granted made them "slaves," too; she wrote, "I have a strong impression that the colored people and the women are to have a day of prosperity and triumph over their oppressors. We must patiently wait and quietly hope; but not keep too much 'in the quiet.' Who would be free, themselves must strike the blow."

Abigail did not suffer lightly those who paid only lip service to abolition. She wrote to William Still in 1858, ". . . oh that people, rich people, would remember them instead of spending so much on themselves; and those, too, who are not called rich, might, if there was only a willing mind, give too of their abundance." She often begged her friends and neighbors for a dollar or two and then made up the rest herself. In a letter to William Still in 1856, she wrote of her efforts to collect money from within the Quaker community: "I have tried to beg something for them, but have not got much; one of our neighbors, S. W. Acton, gave me three dollars for them; I added enough to make ten, which thee will find inside." She asked merchants to donate cheap cloth, then sewed relentlessly with dozens of her friends to outfit the slaves for the cold Northern winters. She herself often went about in rags that were said to cover her no better than the clothing the slaves wore. But as the Civil War raged on, the population became even poorer. New Jersey was required to raise a $100,000 tax, which, said Abigail, "will make the people poorer than ever." She knew it would also mean fewer donations to help escaping slaves.

Though it might have seemed so, there was nothing simple about Abigail. She had a keen, prophetic mind and recognized instantly the self-serving actions of people and government. Her hope for an end to slavery was tempered by her realistic insight into human nature, and this extended even as far as President Abraham Lincoln. In 1861 she wrote bitterly to McKim about Northern political leaders: "I don't believe they care anything about the poor slaves; if the country could have peace and prosperity with slavery, they would scarcely move a finger to remove it." Abigail's perspicacity was born out by Lincoln's letter to Horace Greeley in 1862, wherein he wrote: "If I could save the Union without freeing any slave, I would do it." Even after the Emancipation Proclamation was issued, Abigail commented that although she had read the president's proclamation with thankfulness and rejoicing, she did not feel satisfied with it. She expected that slavery would be a long time in dying, even after receiving the "fatal stroke."

Abigail lived to see the end of the Civil War and the passage of the Thirteenth Amendment in 1865, which freed the slaves she had worked to save for more than thirty years. But at age seventy-three, her health began to fail. In the early morning of November 2, 1867, she died at home. True to form, she insisted in her will that much of her clothing and goods be given to the poor. Her nephew, William Woodnutt, noted in his diary that, "the poor have lost a friend."

Abigail lived her entire life in the same house in the same town, never traveled outside her neighborhood, never married or had children, made no speeches, and wrote no books. But her ceaseless, unselfish humanitarianism saved thousands of lives when no one else would help. And in her quiet way she helped change the course of history. William Still said she "worked for the slave as a mother would work for her children." Perhaps poet Sarah Forten captured Abigail's feelings for justice best when in 1837 she wrote:

> "We are thy sisters; God has truly said,
> That of one blood the nation He has made . . .
> Our skins may differ, but from thee we claim,
> A sister's privilege, and a sister's name."

LILLY MARTIN SPENCER

1822–1902

Virtuoso Painter of the Familiar

"*You* may think . . . that my fame does me a great deal of good, but . . . fame is as hollow and brilliant as a soap bubble, it is all colors outside, and nothing worth kicking at inside," wrote thirty-six-year-old Lilly Martin Spencer to her parents. She had spent all day at her easel. Tirelessly, she labored to perfect her masterpiece, the *Children of Marcus L. Ward*, her fluent brushwork testament to the years of practice. She hoped this would be a great work of art, that the latest critical praise given her would be prophetic.

But, it seemed, no matter how many accolades she earned, the struggle to survive continued unabated. Too many children, too many bills, and never enough money, no matter how many pictures she painted or how many prints were made from those pictures. Now, worst of all, she was forced to take time away from her painting to do the thing she had sworn she would never do—color photographs of her own work. Her husband, Benjamin, while a loving and tender mate, played the role of muse and servant to her work and nursemaid to their children. It was she, and only she, who could feed the growing family.

Lilly Martin Spencer, self-portrait

Angelique Marie, called Lilly, was born on November 26, 1822, to Gilles Marie Martin and Angelique Perrine LePetit Martin, natives of Brittany, France, who had emigrated to the United States. Lilly's parents were "forward thinkers," though their intention to set up a utopian cooperative of five or six families never came to be. Still, their active interest in such social movements as temperance, abolition, and women's suffrage informed their upbringing of Lilly and her two brothers and sister. When Lilly was eleven, her parents left New York to escape a cholera outbreak and settled in Marietta, Ohio, where her father became a French teacher at the Marietta Collegiate Institute and Western Teacher's Seminary. With his wife, he also farmed and schooled his children at home. Lilly's parents were highly educated (her father had studied for the priesthood and her mother was educated in a French convent) and had a large library of classics, including Shakespeare, Pope, Rousseau, and Locke. Both Gilles and Angelique Martin were extremely supportive of any endeavor Lilly chose to pursue, and her obvious early talent in art was encouraged and promoted, especially by her father. This was highly unusual for the day and may have come from the Martins' origins in France at a time of freethinking revolutionary fervor and the admission of women to the French Academy. While in her midteens, Lilly's efforts to "decorate the plaster walls of her family's house with full-length charcoal likenesses of the entire household," including drawings of children, animals, and couples making love, were encouraged by her parents. The Martin home became something of a tourist attraction, and the local newspaper described the drawings as "shaded and finished in the most exquisite manner." Lilly is described at this time as "a strong fervent energetic child . . . wild as the deer on the hills and as full of joy and gladness as the grey squirrel that bounded from limb to limb." Lilly was a lucky girl to have had the parents she did at a time when the ideal daughter was demure, timid, quiet, and docile. Few girls were encouraged to follow their dreams.

Eventually Lilly was tutored by local artists Sala Bosworth and Charles Sullivan and at the age of nineteen held the first exhibition of her paintings. The daytime admission fee of twenty-five cents and evening fee of thirty-seven cents would be used to further her art education. The catalog of the exhibition listed fourteen paintings, with themes from literature as well as romance, and the good-natured sentimentality of the works foreshadowed the style of most of the major works of her career. The editor of the *Cincinnati Chronicle* gushed over this "most astonishing instance of precocity and triumph over difficulty in the arts" and suggested that Lilly would be "a fit subject for the patronage" of Nicholas Longworth, a wealthy lover of the arts and a benefactor of many well-known western artists. Longworth evidently agreed, for he wrote that "a new genius has sprung up at . . . a farmhouse in the shape of a French girl. . . . She is entirely self-taught [and] excells in attitudes and designs." Longworth's interest was the beginning of a lasting friendship between the two.

In spite of Longworth's urging and offer of financial assistance, Lilly decided not to go east to study art in Boston, where she would have learned technique by copying the old masters. Instead, with her father she moved to Cincinnati to study in what was then a western cultural milieu complete with an Academy of Fine Arts. Within a month of her arrival in Cincinnati, Lilly had a second exhibition of her work. Again, Longworth offered to send her for more formal training, this time to Europe. Again, she refused. Perhaps she didn't want to spend the next seven years copying European works. Perhaps she agreed with the philosophy that it was better to paint with a naive eye. Regardless, her decision certainly affected both the quality and subject matter of her paintings for the rest of her life.

"I work at my painting from morning 'til night," she wrote to her mother, and she complained that Cincinnati was "literally full of portrait painters who are set up with their signs, advertisements, and all that, but I shall beat them all, I hope one day." After a year, Lilly's father left her alone in Cincinnati to make an independent life and career. This was quite a gesture of confidence on his part toward the nineteen-year-old girl and an amazing act for the time.

Lilly painted portraits for money, and she observed life rather than taking rigorous formal art lessons. In time she came to regret her lack of training in anatomy and drawing. In 1842 she did take instruction from John Insco Williams, who had studied with Thomas Sully and Russell Smith at the Pennsylvania Academy of Fine Arts. Although she probably learned technical skills and color knowledge from Williams, she soon surpassed her teacher in portraiture. And, surprisingly, although she was female in a profession made up almost totally of men and pursuing a "serious" art career when the mores of the time allowed women only to pursue art as a genteel domestic accomplishment, she found plenty of support and encouragement from her male peers. Perhaps her ebullient personality and strong sense of self-worth played a part in that acceptance. In spite of constant financial struggles, within several years Lilly had established herself as a leading portrait painter in Cincinnati.

On August 24, 1844, Lilly married English immigrant Benjamin Rush Spencer. It was a true love match. More than that, it was a marriage far ahead of its time. Benjamin, after briefly dabbling in a few professions, gave up working to devote himself to supporting Lilly's painting and to taking care of the children and home. Chronic shortages of money often strained the growing family (eventually to number thirteen children, although only seven lived to adulthood), but through it all, Lilly and Benjamin remained happy with each other. No doubt Lilly could never have "had it all" without Benjamin's help. Her colleagues were concerned that marriage would put an end to Lilly's career, for one of them wrote to her that he was "glad to hear you determine to stick to painting. . . . I was fearful matrimony would put an end to painting—I hope not." Lilly's paintings from this time show a flat commercialism that belied her later skill with the brush, but her drawings and sketches show development in anatomy and composition. One, a highly detailed study titled *My Poor Sweet Little Angelica*, shows Lilly and Benjamin's first child in death in 1846 or 1847. The delicate pencil lines drawn on a soft cream paper are remarkable for their detail. Lilly wrote the following inscription in the lower right-hand corner:

> "She took the cup of life to sip
> but bitter t'was to drain
> She meekly put it from her lip
> and went to sleep again."

Although the piece seems maudlin today, posthumous portraits of children (and later, photographs) were not unusual in a time of high infant mortality. A Mr. Aspinall requested that Lilly sketch the "precious face" of his daughter, who had died the previous evening. And a family whose four-year-old had just died commissioned Lilly's portrait of *Daughter of Robert P. Barnard*.

The struggle for money continued through 1847, prompting Benjamin to paint stereoscopic views for "magic lanterns" (popular parlor entertainments, magic lanterns were reflecting boxes with prismatic lenses that projected images from glass slides onto a screen) and to prepare the canvas and make the frames for Lilly's paintings. Lilly complained that she had not sold a single portrait or had a single commission that year. But things began looking up when Lilly became involved with the Western Art Union, an enterprise modeled after the American Art Union in New York. The object of such unions was to bring art to the American public and thereby increase sales for artists. For a small sum, subscribers received an annual engraving of a major painting by an American artist plus the opportunity to win an original work of art in a lottery drawing held once a year. The works purchased for the lottery were selected and exhibited prior to the drawings. In this way, local artists received exposure, were provided studio space, and were eventually written about in monthly art periodicals.

Within a short time, genre scenes and native landscapes made up three-fourths of the work distributed through the Union. Lilly's painting *Life's Happy Hour* was chosen as the first premium print given to subscribers in 1849. Though she was not happy with the engraver's rendering of her work, she must have been thrilled that her association with the Union had brought increased attention to it. She was now known in New York, and she and Benjamin decided to move there in the early fall of 1848. This move would open a world of possibilities for Lilly's development as a portrait and genre painter.

"When we came to New York I found myself so inferior to most of the artists here that . . . I would have to [make] the closest study of almost every part of my art. . . ." wrote Lilly to her mother in 1850. She noted that she was determined to "study everything I had neglected to study when a girl—perspective and all." Lilly painted all day long as well as spending time with her family. In the evenings she took drawing classes at the National Academy of Design as well as observed the work of other artists who had trained in Europe and were rendering the most realistic scenes and portraits. All this created a noticeable improvement in Lilly's painting.

Fortunately the training and observation only served to improve her skills and didn't refine her technique to the detriment of her eye. Lilly's paintings soon achieved an intimacy not unlike the best work of the finest Dutch painters of domestic scenes. Lilly used her own family as models more and more, picturing them engaged in such homey activities as baking, marketing, and putting children to bed. This concentration on domestic humor and sentiment corresponded perfectly with the public's (especially the middle class's) taste in art. Lilly could not (and would not) paint fast enough to satisfy the growing demand for domestic scenes. A friend from Cincinnati wrote:

"The question then arises why you have not sold many more pictures—it is only because instead of two pictures of your peculiar 'genre' you have not had twenty. The plain truth is that pictures remarkable for Maternal, infantine & feminine, expressions, . . . constitute your triumphs, according to popular estimations. . . . I much regret that you have not followed my advice in making repetitions of them all. They would have sold at your own prices as fast as you made them."

It was generally believed that women were not sensual enough to be great artists. Most women, including Lilly, accepted the idea that truly female art was feminine, delicate, dainty, small, and soft-voiced, concerning itself with intimate domestic scenes, especially mothers and children. However, Lilly did not, like some other women, boast of keeping her feminine role sacrosanct and placing her family above her work. Lilly's work always came first.

We can only imagine her struggle. As with all artists, she labored to find her own authenticity, but society pressed her to bow to the dictates of others. And in her anxiety to have her work accepted, Lilly, like other nineteenth-century women painters, "falsified her own perceptions and overstated emotional experiences." Much of Lilly's work is "precious," sentimental, cloyingly sweet, and anatomically stiff. It fit in with the artistic presumptions of the time. Yet one look at her monumental painting of the Ward children proves that Lilly, when she stepped out of the nursery, could paint what is now recognized as a significant example of nineteenth-century art, no matter her gender.

Lilly followed her friend's advice and for the remainder of her life devoted herself to domestic scenes. Her own carpets, utensils, and furniture figure prominently in all her genre paintings, and her skill at isolating familiar and common moments endeared her work to an increasing audience. Lilly's descendants confirm that Benjamin helped his wife by painting some backgrounds on her canvases as well as acting as her business agent, negotiating sales and exhibitions of her work. Lilly wrote to her parents that Benjamin was obliged to care for and comfort a child with fever while she kept "constantly at my portrait" in hopes of eliciting other commissions from its success.

Lilly's output throughout the 1850s and 1860s included a remarkable series of drawings based on characters from Hamlet, reflecting the background in classical literature she had received from her parents during her youth. Many of Lilly's paintings were purchased by William Schaus, a New York agent for the French firm of Goupil, Vibert & Company. The paintings were sent to Paris, where they served as a basis for lithographs, often hand-colored in factories. Most of these were then sent back to the United States to be bought by an eager public. The only money Lilly received was from the initial sale of her paintings. She received no payment for the lithographs, but they helped enormously to spread her name. Two of the most successful lithographs based on Lilly's work were *Power of Fashion* and *Height of Fashion.* In them, black children are depicted as innocent and gleeful as they mimic the pretensions of their elders. Another extremely successful lithograph was *Shake Hands?* (now in the Ohio Historical Society in Columbus). It bears the hallmark of so much of Lilly's best work, intimate and friendly, as a maid, interrupted during her bread making, offers to shake hands with the viewer. The *Cosmopolitan Art Journal* wrote of this painting: "Perhaps no picture painted in this country is better fitted for popular appreciation. It reminds us constantly of the incomparable pictures by the Flemish artists."

Lilly also excelled at painting gorgeous still lifes and animals, many of which were family pets; she captured life's small moments in vivid detail and with gentle humor in such works as *Domestic Happiness, The First Step, The Gossips,* and *Fi! Fo! Fum!,* a tender portrait of Benjamin and two of their children. In contrast to the good-natured portrayal of family life in most of her paintings, Lilly did paint one remarkable animal study, *The Forsaken,* in which a starving mother dog is contrasted with her healthy puppies. This type of "moral" work was rare for Lilly. In most instances the life she portrayed was the stuff of "women's" magazines and fantasy domestic life. It was simply impossible to keep her ebullient personality, enthusiastic nature, and happiness as a mother from coloring everything she painted.

In spite of her fame, Lilly's family constantly struggled to make ends meet. With the invention of the daguerreotype and other photographic methods, portrait commissions decreased. In 1856 she wrote to her mother: "Photographing has allmost entirely destroyed that branch, for they can furnish two or three pictures of the lowest price, that an artist is obliged to ask for painting a portrait in the ordinary way." In an effort to escape the high cost of living in New York City, as well as to satisfy the need for more family and work space, Lilly and her family moved to Newark, New Jersey. It was here that her connection with Nicholas Longworth and his family was to continue and flourish.

The Spencers settled in a house on High Street, and Lilly tried to figure out how to support her growing family on the paltry sums she received from selling her paintings, "notwithstanding my big reputation as they call it," she wrote to her parents. The house belonged to Marcus Ward, nephew of her patron, Nicholas Longworth, connoisseur of the arts and, eventually, governor of the state, and it included a studio in the back of the garden where Lilly could work. Lilly had agreed, as partial payment for the house, to provide three paintings of Ward's children and his wife. Lilly's painting of Marcus Ward's children ranks as one of her finest, and it certainly stands with the best of portraiture of that time. As her parents had done, Lilly and Benjamin raised chickens and farmed a garden for sustenance. And, carrying on the "free" tradition of her own parents, Lilly and Benjamin allowed their children to use the walls of the house for their own artistic pursuits.

The tragedy of the Civil War touched Lilly, too, and many of the paintings she did throughout this period reflect a serious preoccupation with the plight of the soldier as well as the family left waiting at home. One of her most famous works was *The War Spirit At Home: Celebrating the Victory of Vicksburg.* Upon first viewing of this domestic scene, all seems serene as children celebrate with happy faces. A closer inspection, however, reveals deep despair and somber awareness of the emotional and physical toll of war playing across the faces of the women. During this period, three more children were born to Lilly and Benjamin. In spite of the strain this must have caused on the family's finances, Lilly, with her customary good humor and optimism, wrote to her parents: "I am a master at modeling as well as painting babies. . . . You may wonder, dear Mother that I do not feel moor [sic] down hearted at having another responsibility which I hope not to lose while he is small, but look at it poetically and what Mother with her heart aright will be sorry to see her baby's face . . . and as what is done, can't be undone . . . we must endure, we may as well do it cheerfully as sorrowfully."

Two years after the initial rental agreement with Marcus Ward, Lilly passed on the option to purchase the property and moved to 294 High Street in Newark. Lilly continued producing genre paintings of home and hearth, and her prints continued to be wildly popular with the public. One of her most well-known domestic scenes was *The Picnic on the Fourth of July*. During a family outing on the Passaic River, Father falls off a swing while Mother's arms reach out to him. Upon closer inspection, these central characters are revealed to be Lilly and Benjamin. Surrounding figures observe the detailed scene with amusement—wine spills onto the dress of a woman nearby, and a child helps his father to his feet. The rich colors, lush depiction of the landscape, and the vivid portrayal of the characters all combine to make this a work of lasting appeal, typical of the Rustic Romanticism so admired in the mid-nineteenth century.

There were changes in the wind. Wealthy patrons, fickle as always, decided that European paintings indicated a more "serious" appreciation of "art," and the market soon became overstocked with foreign paintings. Post–Civil War boomtimes meant more upper-middle class and wealthy people eager to show their "taste" by purchasing European art for their drawing rooms. Domestic scenes, once so popular, lost their appeal after the somber realities of war. Along with these factors came an increased desire for paintings containing allegorical and historical rather than hearth and home scenes. Lilly's work did not fit the new tastes at all.

During this time, Lilly worked assiduously on a massive painting titled *Truth Unveiling Falsehood*. Although Lilly considered it her "masterpiece," no doubt because it had a "serious" allegorical message, it pales in every way compared with her magnificent portraits and still lifes. But it is understandable that Lilly would want to refute certain critics who had savaged her work as full of "grinning housemaids" instead of reflecting a "tenderer deeper conception of humanity" that it was a woman's responsibility to bring to art. She herself had always believed that art should catalyze moral improvement and that "a fine painting has a beautiful power over the human passions." It was predicted that *Truth Unveiling Falsehood* would "cover her name with glory" as well as bring her riches and financial independence. She did receive a gold medal for it, issued on the occasion of its exhibit at the Philadelphia Centennial in 1876. And Senator William Sprague of New Jersey offered to purchase it, as did John Wanamaker, who is said to have offered $20,000 for the painting. But no evidence exists that the work, which Lilly refused to sell for the sums offered during her lifetime, ever brought an improvement in her financial situation. Once this painting was completed, she returned to domestic subjects and did not stray again.

Some of Lilly's finest paintings, including *We Both Must Fade*, a portrait of a Mrs. Fithian now in the National Collection of Fine Arts, Smithsonian Institution, were exhibited in the Women's Pavilion of the Centennial Exhibition in Philadelphia in 1876. According to correspondence, Lilly would have preferred that her work be shown in the main exhibition area.

In an 1879 auction catalog, Lilly was listed as "deceased," a poignant metaphor for the disappearance from public view of her work by that time. During that year the Spencers moved to Highland, New York. Shortly thereafter, Benjamin broke his hip, resulting in his becoming permanently disabled. Despite a number of retrospectives of her work, in a continuing struggle to raise funds to support her family, in January 1890 Lilly auctioned fourteen of her paintings, for which the highest price received was $10. One month later, in February, her beloved Benjamin died.

Now alone, Lilly moved back to New York City. Throughout her seventies, her passion for painting sustained as well as supported her, even though she was sometimes forced to barter paintings in order to put bread on the table. Indeed, Lilly never stopped painting, continuing to develop her skills in technique and composition right up until her death on the afternoon of May 22,

1902. True to form, the seventy-nine-year-old artist had spent that morning at her easel.

Lilly Martin Spencer was one of those fortunate beings born with a jovial spirit and a perpetually optimistic outlook. The strength of her nature, her natural ebullience, a sturdy physicality, and well-developed self-esteem enabled her to find the positive in every situation and to keep doing the thing she loved best, in spite of cultural and financial pressures that would have daunted most other women of her time.

On one hand, she represented the life of a traditional woman, with a husband and thirteen children whom she treasured. The other side of Lilly revealed an independent and organized woman who handled family life and personal affairs in an extremely progressive way.

More than a million prints of Lilly's paintings were reproduced during the middle of the nineteenth century. Her work dealt not only with domestic scenes but also with war, literary characters, important historical events, and allegorical themes. The most important *female* artist of her era, she was also one of the most important artists of the nineteenth century. Her finest works hang in museums throughout the world, including the Smithsonian Institution and as part of the permanent collection of the Newark Museum. A more fitting tribute could not have been written than this homage by a contemporary: "Let Men . . . know that with the skill of her hands and the power of her head, she sustains a family. . . . Aye, sustains them a thousandfold better than she could have done with the needle or the washtub, and gives out to the world besides, the rich treasures which become the rays of sunshine in many a heart and home. Heaven bless thee, Lilly Martin Spencer."

ANTOINETTE BROWN BLACKWELL

1825–1921

America's First Ordained Woman Minister

*T*wenty-eight-year-old Antoinette's hands shook and her heart fluttered as she took the podium in New York's Metropolitan Hall. Everywhere she looked she saw a sea of clergymen. Where were her women friends? She needed to see them, to feel their support. For in spite of the fact that this temperance meeting had been declared open to all without respect to age, gender, color, or condition, she knew it was not. She also knew that, determined as she was to speak, it was a risky business for a woman to dare speak in public. Calmly and strongly, she began: "Every woman feels a deep and double interest [in the cause of temperance]." Instantly, the angry crowd of ministers drowned out her voice, shouting, stamping, and pounding on the floor with their canes. "This is not the appropriate sphere of woman," they yelled. "You trespass on masculine grounds!" "Silence!" "Go home to your husband and be quiet!" "Where is your Christian decency and propriety!" Looking out into the crowd of angry men, Antoinette was filled with a feeling of power and calm. Gazing into flashing, defiant

Antoinette Brown Blackwell

eyes, she felt a spirit stronger than the violent mob. Steeling herself against the threats and insults, her backbone firm and her chin raised defiantly, Antoinette knew that at that moment, not the combined powers of earth and hell could have tempted her to do anything but stand firm.

Antoinette Louisa (Nette) Brown was born on May 20, 1825, on her family's farm in Henrietta, New York. The year that Antoinette was born was an auspicious one due to significant social, industrial, and economic change. The Erie Canal was completed and opened, a critical factor in the transformation of commerce that influenced the whole country. Increased trade, widespread industrialization, new influxes of immigrants, westward migration, and growth of cities with its attendant increase in crime and urban ills all impacted daily life. The country was ripe for change, and Antoinette was born into its waiting arms.

Antoinette's mother, Abigail Morse Brown, a descendant of six generations of New England farmers, was born in southern Massachusetts in 1793. She attended school to learn to read and keep household accounts. Antoinette wrote of her mother: "She was a natural business woman of much executive ability, able to carry through any undertaking. If she had lived in modern times she would certainly have been a power." She married Antoinette's father, Joseph Brown, also a sixth-generation New Englander, in 1810, when she was seventeen and he was twenty-five, and they set up housekeeping on a farm in Connecticut. Joseph Brown, a farmer and justice of the peace, was a supporter of all the liberal causes of the day, including women's rights and abolition. Nine years later Abigail and Joseph joined a steady stream of pioneers heading for western New York and settled in the area around Rochester, buying one hundred acres of land with a two-room log cabin on it. The Browns prospered, and the family continued to grow. Abigail bore a child about every two years, and by 1833 there were ten children in the family, Antoinette being the seventh. In 1830 the family moved from the cramped cabin to a new stone house down the road. This home had a large open attic where the children could sleep. These were happy years, filled with such rural pastimes as cheese and candle making, fruit drying, yarn dying, pickling, wheat farming, and even an experiment in cultivating silkworms.

The only person in the household who considered herself a committed Christian was Antoinette's grandmother. Antoinette and the other children spent many hours in the older woman's room, listening to her read from the Bible and talking with her about it. Antoinette was close to her grandmother and attributed much of her thoughtfulness "to this dear" woman. It is not insignificant that Antoinette's first religious teacher was a woman.

Western New York was a hotbed of religious excitement during the first part of the nineteenth century. Traveling evangelical preachers exhorted listeners to moral perfection, and experimental religious communities sprang up everywhere. In the rapidly changing times, religion offered stability and great comfort. Many churches embraced positive social change and supported the building momentum for abolition, temperance, and equal rights. One extremely popular evangelist, Charles Grandison Finney, who stressed personal conversion along with working toward a more perfect society, had an enormous influence in the Rochester area and on the Brown family. Antoinette first heard him when she was six years old, and his dual commitment to personal as well as societal perfection had a profound effect on her religious beliefs as well as those of her parents and siblings. At the age of nine, Antoinette spoke out at church, declared her faith, and was accepted as a member by her local Congregational meetinghouse. Most important for her spiritual development, neither Antoinette's church nor her parents stressed punishment but taught children to envision God as a "friendly presence." For Antoinette, God was as accessible as the green grass. The death of her grandmother when Antoinette was nine only confirmed her perception of a loving God, as Antoinette's grandmother was reported to have said just before she died, "I have been talking with the angels and they are all around me now."

Antoinette excelled at school, and her writing ability appeared early. Her family was a loving and happy one where her abilities were appreciated and encouraged. Yet, at the same time, she could see that her parents were stuck in their roles by circumstances beyond their control and that society's ideas of women's proper sphere would not work for her.

The educational system in Henrietta was similar to those in many other rural places. Local teachers, many of whom were recent graduates of the nearby school, conducted classes. William and Sam, Antoinette's brothers, taught her for one year. It was Sam who kindled in her a deep interest in science and nature that, in her own words, "had a considerable effect on my subsequent life." When Antoinette was thirteen, she graduated from the district school she had attended for ten years and joined her siblings at Monroe Country Academy, the first secondary school in the county. During the winter the students often stayed at the school, cooking for themselves and feeding and teaching the younger students. Even at this young age, the children were considered mature and responsible, and no thought was given to the fact that boys and girls shared the dormitory-like space. Victorian proprieties were not a part of country living.

Antoinette graduated from the academy in 1840. The next spring, at the age of sixteen, she became a teacher at a nearby district school. The following summer she moved to Genesee to teach. She was paid $1.50 a week plus board. She gave most of her salary to her parents but saved $1.00 back to buy writing paper. Antoinette knew that teaching was one of the few jobs available to unmarried women and that she could have made teaching her career, but she wanted more and neither chose nor enjoyed domestic chores. Many of those against female education feared that exposure to ideas would make women unfit for domestic and social duties. In Antoinette's case, it is likely that she saw her mother's ceaseless labor and rebelled against it. In any case, during this time Antoinette's desire to become a minister crystallized. It was not unusual for young women at this time to be religious, but it *was* unusual for them to set their sights on actual ordainment. Women were not expected to become public leaders of religious communities. No woman anywhere had ever been ordained as a priest or minister, and the notion of a woman in the pulpit was considered ludicrous—if not sacrilegious. Only Quaker women could speak at their meetinghouses, where all members contributed on an equal basis and ordination was not a prerequisite. But Antoinette had shown an exceptional capacity for spiritual leadership, and she seems to have taken it for granted that the call was not limited by gender.

In order to become a minister, Antoinette needed more education. But most colleges would not accept women, and women's colleges had yet to be formed. The few postsecondary schools that did exist taught only moral self-improvement and social skills, really training for a life as a wife and mother. So Antoinette set her sights on Oberlin Collegiate Institute, far away in Ohio. Although Oberlin had some inequities that Antoinette would encounter later on, it was a progressive institution for its time, granting degrees to women, men, and individuals from different races and supporting critical social issues such as abolition. Indeed, Oberlin was well known as a hotbed of antislavery sentiment and forward-thinking ideas. Charles Grandison Finney, her family's spiritual leader, was now president. He was to influence Antoinette's life at Oberlin, just as he had the lives of her family years before. Most important to Antoinette, Oberlin admitted women to study with men at the college level. She hoped eventually to study theology there. But although Antoinette's family was supportive of women going to college, they needed her at home to help her mother, and Antoinette's father was concerned about being able to afford the tuition. Not one to be deterred, Antoinette bided her time; she taught for three more years, saving her earnings and dreaming of the day when she could begin her studies.

Those three years were a difficult time for the Brown family. Antoinette's mother was often sick and worn out by childbearing. Her beloved brother, Sam, died of tuberculosis a few days after her eighteenth birthday. Her closest sister, Ophelia, died of the same disease the following October, and two older sisters died within the next two years. Her faith in God as a merciful being must have been sorely tested.

Finally, in the spring of 1846, Antoinette set out for Oberlin, making the 300-mile trip by barge, steamer, and stagecoach in three days. It was on this trip that Antoinette first heard the name of Lucy Stone, a woman who would play an essential part in Antoinette's story for the rest of her life. She was warned, however, that she should not become too friendly with her, as Lucy was "much too talkative on the subject of woman's rights." True to form, Antoinette said nothing at the time but made up her mind to know more of this woman.

The town of Oberlin was still a pioneer settlement, ankle deep in mud and running wild with hens, hogs, and cattle. Sanitation was nonexistent, and cholera, pneumonia, and tuberculosis were constant problems, as Antoinette would learn firsthand. Originally founded by a group of ministers and their families, Oberlin was dedicated to creating a new community, a mixture of liberal religion, practical training, and reform politics. A month after its founding in 1833, Oberlin was filled with an influx of white and black students who had left Lane Seminary near Cincinnati after a dispute over the abolition of slavery. By the time Antoinette arrived, more than 10 percent of the town's people were black or mulatto escapees (via the Underground Railroad) and free Negroes. Oberlin expected all students to share in the manual labor that contributed to the college's well-being. However, women were expected to work at washing and other domestic chores, while men completed outdoor tasks. Antoinette's first job was washing dishes in the boarding hall, but she was soon promoted from domestic chores to teaching drawing, much more to her liking!

Antoinette had little time for loneliness. Every morning she rose at five o'clock and after dressing and cleaning her room spent half an hour in private meditation. This was followed by breakfast and prayers, classes, and studying from seven in the morning to five at night, with an hour break for midday dinner. She attended religious lectures or sermons on Tuesday and Thursday afternoon and prayer in the chapel every evening. She studied every night and was in her room by eight o'clock with her candle blown out by ten. Among the subjects Antoinette studied were Greek, Latin, Hebrew, mathematics, astronomy, chemistry, geology, biology, logic, and rhetoric.

Many young women had come to Oberlin to obtain an education in preparation for work as public speakers, but they soon discovered that the school was as biased against them as the rest of society. Women at Oberlin were prohibited from speaking in mixed groups and from participation in discussions or debates. As this training was primarily a prerequisite for entering the ministry or law, it was considered unnecessary for women. The education of women was to be an enhancement of their natural roles as wives and mothers—nothing more. Antoinette and her friends were bitterly disappointed by Oberlin's policy, so when third-year student Lucy Stone challenged the rules by speaking publicly at a celebration in honor of the tenth anniversary of West Indian slave emancipation and was summarily reprimanded, her example encouraged her classmates, among them Antoinette, to take similar action. They revitalized the Ladies Literary Society, where they could train themselves in secret for public speaking. If they could not receive formal training, they would develop skills on their own! Among the subjects they covered was a report on the Seneca Falls women's rights convention in 1848. As Antoinette's friendship with Lucy Stone deepened, they began writing to each other, a practice they kept up their entire lives and one that resulted in almost fifty years of letters between them. It was in the winter of 1846–47 that their friendship deepened into an enduring love. Antoinette, desperate for funds, was teaching at a private institute in Michigan during a school break and was no doubt lonely and homesick. Her attention focused on Lucy, and it is certain they were forever bound by an emotional intensity few marriages can match. That winter Antoinette wrote to Lucy: "We believed no more things in common than any other of my classmates . . . & yet I loved you more than all the rest together."

In addition to loving friendship, Lucy provided a wonderful intellectual foil for Antoinette. They disagreed often on tactics. Antoinette was still committed to organized Christianity. Lucy had left the church because it accepted slavery and opposed women speaking in public. When Antoinette shared her intent to become a minister with Lucy, her friend declared angrily: "You will never be allowed to do this. You will never be allowed to stand in a pulpit, nor to preach in a church, and certainly you can never be ordained." Typically, Antoinette's final answer to Lucy was "I am going to do it." That spring Lucy left Oberlin to begin a career as a public speaker on abolition. Antoinette remained at Oberlin to begin her study of theology.

Antoinette's time at Oberlin was difficult. The college was reluctant to accept female students into the theology program, believing that women should not be allowed to become career preachers. Yet the school charter specifically stated that students could not be denied admission to a course of study because of gender. Finally Antoinette was permitted to enter the program without participation in class discussions or recitation. To her eternal gratitude, Finney, the family's old friend, supported Antoinette in her attempt to change this rule. An assigned essay on the Biblical passages that forbade women to speak forced Antoinette to use all her training and education to justify her position. Her final paper was considered good enough for publication in the *Oberlin Quarterly Review*. Although she thought that the church's stance on women speaking in public was wrong, Antoinette made a determined effort to integrate orthodox Christianity with her beliefs on reform politics and women's rights. She still believed that rational arguments could change others' minds, especially those of the rigid clergy, and she was unhappy that her dear friend Lucy did not support her theological studies. Lucy had written, "Yet *my own dear Nette* is spending *three* precious years of her life's young prime, wading through that deep slough, from the stain of which she can never wash herself and by which, I *fear*, her vision will be so clouded that she can only see *men* through creeds. . . ." During her second winter, Antoinette suffered so greatly from ambivalence about her goals that she became ill. Her health problems were also due, no doubt, to the lack of sanitation in the Oberlin community. Still she persevered, returning to Oberlin at the beginning of 1850. Her disagreement with Lucy continued as well. Lucy wrote that Oberlin had "trampled" Antoinette's womanhood and that she had "settled." But Antoinette disagreed, replying that she had returned to Oberlin upon no terms at all. Ever the pragmatist, she wrote to Lucy, "They refused to receive me into the Institution. I came back to study Theology and get knowledge. I do get it, they don't interfere." She insisted she had nothing to do with Oberlin conduct or decisions and that when she went out to work she would act honorably regardless of what others thought. But she was angry with Lucy and declared: "I am no more conservative, creed-loving, time-serving or bigoted than I was three years since. I am no less of a free thinker or independent actor."

Lucy and Antoinette's ongoing disagreement reflected larger disagreements in the women's rights and other progressive movements arena. Does one fight from within or without? Should Antoinette stay at Oberlin without formal recognition and seemingly accept their terms, or should she make a political statement by leaving and not get the education she wanted?

She chose the former and graduated from Oberlin at the end of the summer term in 1850 at the age of twenty-five. She was allowed no part in the commencement exercises. She was not acknowledged to have actually graduated, as to do that would have meant that Oberlin endorsed her future plans to become a minister. And her name did not appear in official listings of the theological class of 1850 until 1908, when she was awarded an honorary Doctorate of Divinity.

For a few years after Antoinette graduated, she pursued a career as a lecturer, giving speeches on temperance, abolition, and women's rights throughout New York, Ohio, Pennsylvania, and New England. She attended and spoke at many early women's rights conventions, including the Worcester Women's Rights Convention—the first such event to be billed as a national gathering—and one in New York in 1852. In 1853 she attended women's rights conventions in New York City and Cleveland and was appointed as a delegate to the World's Temperance Convention in New York City. At that convention she was shouted down by a hostile audience and ultimately expelled because she had attempted to speak.

On September 15, 1853, the First Congregational Church in Butler, New York, ordained her as their pastor, making her the first woman minister of a recognized denomination in the United

States. She received the sum of $300 a year for her service. A large crowd of friends and neighbors braved a huge downpour to witness this historic event. For Antoinette it was a solemn occasion, one wherein she felt she had breached the "great wall of custom" she'd once described to Lucy. Not all was rosy, however. After an article about her ordination appeared in the *New York Tribune,* the public was aghast. Some people even denied that she had been ordained and attempted to take that honor away from her.

Antoinette preached twice on Sunday and carried out full pastoral duties, including visiting the sick and tending to the needs of her congregation. Shortly after she was ordained, she became the first woman to officiate at a marriage ceremony—the wedding of the daughter of Rhoda deGarmo, a fellow women's rights supporter.

Despite her precedent-setting achievement, Antoinette was having doubts about her first ministerial assignment and about the denomination itself. She could not support the Congregational Church's belief in the concepts of original sin, eternal punishment, or predestination. She found less and less certainty in the authority of the Bible and "found that the whole groundwork of [her] faith had dropped away from [her]." Some members of Antoinette's congregation made requests that she felt she could not honor. In one instance she was asked to preach against the mother's sins at the funeral of an illegitimate child and, in another, was requested by the mother of a dying young man to force him to convert on his deathbed by threatening him with hell's fire and brimstone. Antoinette refused; she could not reconcile herself to such a brutal God. She felt lonely and isolated with nowhere to turn to share her increasing doubts, even with her dearest friends or reformer colleagues in the women's rights movement. This emotional strain eventually caused a severe breakdown in her health, and during this time she finally realized that she could not in good conscience remain at her job. She left the Congregational Church in July 1854, less than a year after her ordination, and returned to her parents' home to rest and recuperate.

After regaining her strength Antoinette became active once again, serving as secretary of the National Woman's Rights Convention, giving a series of lectures for the New York Antislavery Society, and traveling with Ernestine L. Rose on a lecture tour of New England and New York. In 1855 Horace Greeley encouraged her to spend some time in New York City's slums and institutions and to write about her observations in the *Tribune.*

Antoinette's personal theology would never be the same after her experience of poverty and mental illness among the poor, especially women. She visited tenements teeming with Irish and German immigrants and asylums for poor and handicapped children on Randall's Island as well as the Tombs. She wrote that her "work among the poor and degraded . . . was so pitiful that it was almost too much . . . to one whose life had hitherto been so sheltered." To Antoinette, "it made the whole world seem a place of shadows and sorrows." Her series of newspaper articles was later published as a book, *Shadows of Our Social System.*

During her travels as a speaker and reformer, Antoinette had often stayed at the Samuel and Hannah Blackwell home in Cincinnati. She felt quite comfortable there and, while having developed a friendship with the young Samuel Blackwell, showed no signs of romantic interest in him. After all, though she respected marriage as an institution, Antoinette had never thought she would marry. She had written to Lucy that she had accepted celibacy as her destiny and that she "would never expect to find a man who would sympathize with [her] feelings and acquiesce in [her] plans." Samuel had visited with Antoinette at her South Butler parish when she was undergoing her most serious doubts, and it was eventually to him that she turned a few years later. "When the early faith seemed wholly lost and the new and stronger belief not yet obtained," she wrote, "there seemed no good reason for not accepting the love and help of a good man." But Antoinette had very clear ideas of the kind of cooperation she expected in a marriage. In a letter to Samuel in 1856, she wrote: "Only leave me free, as free as you are and everyone ought to be, and it is giving up nothing. It will not be so very hard to have a dear quiet own home with one's husband to love and be loved by . . ."

The Blackwell clan that Antoinette married into in January 1855 was an amazing group of people. Samuel's sisters, Elizabeth and Emily Blackwell, were the first two women to have earned medical degrees and to practice medicine in the United States. His older sister, Anna, was the first woman foreign correspondent, and a younger sister, Ellen, was an artist and writer. Samuel's brother, Henry, an abolitionist and suffragist, married Antoinette's dear friend, political activist Lucy Stone. The entire Blackwell family was active and prominent in securing political and legal rights and in expanding educational and professional training for women. At the same time, they were an odd bunch. Very close to one another, they rarely formed intimate relationships outside the family. The five Blackwell sisters never married, and historical documents portray this group of women, as well as Lucy, their sister-in-law, as repelled by any kind of physical closeness, including sexuality.

Antoinette was different and, it seems, the only woman in the Blackwell clan who had a close and satisfying physical relationship with her husband. Indeed, while on speaking tours Antoinette yearned for Samuel and wrote to him: "The truth is I fall in love with you anew every time we separate." Her niece Alice once commented about Antoinette and Samuel that, "such a pair of lovers I never saw." Antoinette's good fortune in growing up in a liberal and loving family stood her in good stead for a marriage partnership of long and tender duration.

Antoinette soon became pregnant with her first child. She looked forward to a houseful of children, much like her own parents' home, but she must also have wondered how she could continue her public work once the baby came. The entire Blackwell clan had decided to move east, and by October Samuel had found a job as a bookkeeper. Shortly after their first child, Florence, was born, Samuel and Antoinette moved to New Jersey, his boyhood home. There they moved into their first house, a tiny building in the middle of Newark. And though they would move from house to house many times, they would make New Jersey their permanent home. Henry and Lucy soon moved to Orange, about 5 miles away, and Antoinette and Lucy continued their shared, now familial, connection on a daily basis, though without the emotional intensity of their years at Oberlin. During this time, Lucy gave birth to Alice Stone Blackwell, who also became Antoinette's friend for life. Soon Antoinette's second child, Mabel, was born but died tragically at three months old from an infection. Antoinette grieved desperately, confiding to Lucy that she found it "hard to quite rally from the unexpected blow." But rally she did, and she and Sam went on to have five more daughters, another of whom died in infancy. Daughters Edith and Ethel became doctors, and Agnes became an artist and teacher. Throughout their marriage, Samuel supported Antoinette's intellectual and reform activities and shared equally in domestic duties. All their daughters were given the double last names of Brown Blackwell.

Perhaps partly to bury her grief at Mabel's death, as well as to gain solace from the work she believed in, Antoinette resumed her lecture schedule with intensity. She and Susan B. Anthony first conducted a speaking tour of upstate New York, and then Antoinette proceeded with her long-planned "New York Experiment," during which she traveled from her home in New Jersey to preach weekly in New York City during the 1859–60 season. In addition, she continued her work as a circuit speaker. During this time Antoinette became associated with many women's rights groups, including the Equal Rights Association, an organization that concentrated on the growing campaign to secure for women the right to vote. She spoke out passionately on behalf of what she believed, spending a great deal of time studying and writing about her causes. She once remarked that writing could accomplish much in "reforming the world."

Ultimately, surrounded as she was by the domestic sphere, Antoinette for the most part gave up public speaking. Household responsibilities certainly weighed heavily and required modifications in her schedule, but home and family were extremely important to Antoinette. Sam shouldered much of the responsibility, sharing chores and child-care tasks, giving a practical face to his belief in marital equality and making it possible for Antoinette to continue her work. As her children grew, she wrote and published many books on science and philosophy, including *Studies in General Science* (1869), wherein she analyzed the new science in relationship to traditional Christian doctrine. She also wrote *The Sexes Throughout Nature* (1875), a refutation of both Charles Darwin's and Herbert Spencer's claims that women contributed less to human evolution than men, *The Physical Basis of Immortality* (1876), *The Philosophy of Individuality* (1893), *The Human Element in Sex* (1894), a novel, and poetry. Ironically, although Antoinette was well educated in theology, by the 1870s she was writing in a completely naturalistic and scientific framework. In all, nine books came from Antoinette's pen, the last finished on her ninetieth birthday!

Although Antoinette continued to be involved in women's rights activities, her devotion to domestic life and liberal religion gave her a broader outlook from that of other women's rights advocates. She hated the petty infighting over platforms and tactics and eschewed rigid rules that eventually resulted in the women's rights movement's split into two suffrage organizations—the American Woman Suffrage Association (AWSA) and the National Woman Suffrage Association (NWSA). Although she remained good friends with the more radical Elizabeth Cady Stanton, Lucretia Mott, and Susan B. Anthony, Antoinette's personal loyalty to Lucy Stone and Henry Blackwell drew her more closely to the more traditional and conservative AWSA. However, she refused to ally herself with either faction. She maintained her support for marriage and organized religion as well as suffrage and equal participation in the political process, focusing more on what she called the moral progress of the universe and such personal issues as education for women, poverty, divorce, health care, and work opportunities.

Antoinette stepped forward into leadership positions where needed. She founded the New Jersey Women's Suffrage Association in 1867. She contributed articles to the *Woman's Journal* and delivered a paper at the first congress of the Association for the Advancement of Women in 1873 as well as serving as its vice president. When Samuel suffered financial reverses in the late 1870s, Antoinette once again took speaking engagements, traveling extensively throughout the country. Later in her life she spoke before the Senate Committee on Woman Suffrage in Washington, D.C., and held a place of honor in the 1911 Fifth Avenue suffrage parade in New York City. At the advanced age of ninety-two, she remained passionately interested in equal rights. She wrote: "As a woman whose husband scorned the idea of an obedient wife . . . I will never give my adherence to an exclusively male-made and a male-administered government in family, in church, or in state. I, who lived and saw the evils of that awful dispensation, and early protested with heart and voice, still protest."

Antoinette's religious leadership remained firm. She preached throughout the United States and officiated at or assisted in religious services at suffrage and other conventions. At the age of seventy-eight, she traveled alone to Palestine to bring back water from the River Jordan to christen her two grandchildren. Most important, she opened up the ministry to women. In 1902 she presided at the funeral service of her old friend, Elizabeth Cady Stanton. And her strong religious beliefs enabled her to salve her grief when, at the age of seventy-five, her intimate friend and sister, Lucy Stone, died of stomach cancer. Antoinette firmly believed in immortality and expected to meet her friend in the future. When Sam, her husband of forty-five years, died after a series of strokes in 1901, Antoinette told her niece, "I feel now that when I go forward I shall go right to him."

In the fall of 1903, Antoinette went to live with her daughter Agnes and Agnes's husband in Elizabeth. Finally she was able to realize one of her most fervent dreams: a parish of her own without the doctrinal restrictions she had rejected many years before. In 1903 she donated land and helped organize the All Souls Unitarian Church in Elizabeth. She conducted services until a new minister was brought forward in 1908 and thereafter bore the title of Minister Emeritus. She preached there once a month until old age overcame her.

In 1920 the Nineteenth Amendment was finally adopted, granting women the right to vote. Local news stories reported that Antoinette Blackwell was the only one of her contemporaries in the suffrage movement to live to experience the triumph of this moment and that, at the next election, voters on a long line at the polling place stood aside to allow the deeply revered older woman to cast her ballot first. Late in November 1921, Antoinette died peacefully in her sleep at the age of ninety-seven.

Despite her public political activity, Antoinette had always thought of herself more as a minister than a scientist or reformer. Indeed, she was known throughout feminist circles as a pioneer who "first opened the door of the American pulpit," but it still remains for today's scholars and future generations to truly recognize the brilliant, steady work Antoinette achieved throughout her lifetime, including her seminal scientific writings and her radical proposals for redistributing work between men and women. As Antoinette wrote in 1914: "Woman's future part in civil, religious, society, and domestic world-making remains to unfold itself."

MARY MAPES DODGE

1830–1905

Creator of Hans Brinker and *St. Nicholas*

Lover of little ones
Up to the end,
Everywhere children now
Mourn for their friend.
—Josephine Daskam Bacon

*F*ifteen thousand panes of glass burst into the air as the magnificent dome of the Crystal Palace in New York City collapsed in ruins. Spectators watched in horror as the entire structure was consumed by fire and all the exhibits were destroyed. On that early October day in 1858, the American Institute's once-promising showcase of invention and industry lay in ruins.

Lizzie's world was collapsing, too. She sat silently in a brocade chair in her apartment below Union Square, listening to the subdued voices of her boys upstairs. What was she to do now? How could someone who loved her and his boys just disappear?

Mary Mapes Dodge

For that was what William had done—just walked out the door on that bleak October evening a little before dark "for a breath of air," he'd said. The table was set for dinner; a fire snapped in the hearth. As the hours ticked by, Lizzie had expected him to throw open the front door any minute, bringing with him the cold rush of fall air. But he never came. The family rallied around her. Day after day they scanned the papers for news of accidental deaths. William's father placed an ad in the *New York Times*, assuring his son that all was fine at home and that he would be welcomed back with open arms. Lizzie's father placed another ad, asking that anyone who might have met a stranger struggling with melancholia contact the family immediately. When there was no answer to that ad, he tried again, offering the information that his son-in-law might now be wandering through the country under slight mental derangement. No reply ever came, and finally Lizzie had to accept the truth. William was not coming back. Perhaps he had accidentally drowned in the unusually high autumn tide. She would never truly know, but the gay and happy life she had loved was over. She was only twenty-eight years old and a widow. Her world had shattered with the same force and swiftness as the beautiful Crystal Palace. Now she must figure out how to support herself and be both mother and father to her two boys—and she must make a plan to pay off the mountain of debt William had incurred. But there was one thing Lizzie absolutely insisted upon: The curtain was to be drawn on her pain and grief. William's disappearance would never be examined, debated, probed, or scrutinized. Neither she nor anyone else in her family would ever speak of it again.

Mary Elizabeth Mapes (Lizzie) was born in New York City on January 26, 1830. Her mother, Sophia Furman Mapes, was an amateur artist and musician, delicate, distractible and, from all descriptions, somewhat fey. Her father, James Jay Mapes, was a brilliant scholar, inventor, and scientist with a magnetic personality who drew friends and acquaintances from far and wide to his home. He had consulted with Lincoln on Civil War campaigns, had invented a method for extracting sap from sugar cane, produced brown sugar in the form we know today, worked on the process that led to the invention of malleable iron, and developed a better pigment for oil painting as well as Mapes dyes. The Mapes and Furman families had known each other over the years, both in New York City and on Long Island, and Sophia and James had been childhood friends prior to their marriage. Lizzie had three sisters, Louise, Sophie, and Kate, and a brother, Charlie. Brilliant though he may have been, James Mapes was seldom able to translate his ideas into profit-making ventures. The family moved frequently, each time to smaller, less-expensive homes. Still, Lizzie's childhood was a "remarkably happy" one, "watched over with loving care," surrounded by grandparents, aunts and uncles, siblings, and devoted parents as well as by some of the most influential thinkers of the day, who came to engage in stimulating intellectual debate with her father. Indeed, Lizzie and her siblings developed intellectual horizons far beyond that of many of their contemporaries. Lizzie wrote of Christmas in the Mapes household: "O, those bursting stockings! And father and mother looking on as we opened parcel after parcel in the early dawn! . . . and while the great blazing wood fire crackled on the nursery fireplace. And then the letter from Santa Claus himself, telling us to be good children always. . . .Well, it was just a real Christmas, and that's all there is to be said."

Lizzie was very close to her father in looks, temperament, and intellect. Deeply influenced by him from an early age, she spent many hours with "Professor" Mapes discussing science and great books. Lizzie and her brother and sisters were all educated at home by a tutor and allowed unlimited access to their father's extensive library. James Mapes believed that children should be exposed to real literature early and often rather than being fed the moralistic pap traditionally reserved for them. Consequently, Lizzie's young mind was inspired by such classic material as the tales of King Arthur and adventure stories such as *Robinson Crusoe* and the *Arabian Nights*. She must have been somewhat of a prodigy, because from the age of eight on she edited her father's publications and helped him document his scientific experiments.

In 1846 New Jersey's farms were failing because of soil depletion, and land was being sold cheaply at auction. James Mapes desperately wanted to buy a piece of land in order to prove that his theory on land renewal through the use of chemical fertilizers had merit. Perennially broke, James had no money for such an investment, but he did have a prospective financial partner in mind. New York lawyer William Dodge III was an acquaintance of James's through his involvement in politics and membership in the St. Nicholas Society. James brought William home to meet his family, and William's eye fell on Lizzie. His intelligent and gentle personality as well as his romanticism appealed to her. Her lovely dark hair and blue eyes combined with her keen intellect and confident personality at the young age of seventeen must have appealed to him. This sheltered girl and the romantic "older" lawyer fell in love, and the fifteen-year difference in their ages did not seem to matter.

An arrangement using a straw man and William's money enabled James to purchase a run-down farm in Waverly, Essex County, now part of Newark. (The farmhouse was near the corner of the present-day intersection of Mapes and Elizabeth Avenues in Newark.) The family's declining fortunes would have led to more marked poverty in New York, but in the country James could preserve his intellectual and scientific environment and support his family at lesser expense—at worst in the guise of shabby gentility. And so in 1848 the family moved to Mapleridge, a three-story mansion with two chimneys and a cupola surrounded by trees. The house had a rambling porch on two sides and lovely gardens. The smell of the sea came from the east, and fields stretched as far as the eye could see toward Irvington. The rugs were worn and the furniture somewhat battered, but no one noticed in a house that vibrated with energy, youth, music, art, books, and such visitors as Horace Greeley, Washington Irving, and William Cullen Bryant. James entertained with his wit and his remarkable stories. Lizzie worked on scientific pamphlets, providing details of her father's numerous experiments and theories; edited her father's new magazine, the *Working Farmer;* and was courted by William. It was a wonderful time, even though James's successful agricultural experiments and his growing prominence as a scientist didn't provide any income.

On September 13, 1851, Lizzie and William were married and went to live with William's large family below Union Square in New York City. Their first child, a son, James, was born in 1852; their second son, Harrington, arrived in 1855. Their lives were prosperous, William was happy, and Lizzie was a serene and loving mother. But dark clouds were gathering.

In August 1857 a sailing ship carrying a huge shipment of gold from California sank. Banks needed that gold to back up failing investments that had caused the American public to panic. Investors were losing heavily in the stock market, and railroads could not pay their debts. Fearing financial ruin, people ran to the banks to withdraw their money, but the banks did not deal in paper currency. They used silver and gold, but because of the sinking it was impossible for the banks to make good on their accounts. All across the country they began to collapse, ultimately leading to a three-year economic depression.

William had borrowed heavily during this period, mortgaging property after property in order to loan his father-in-law money so that James could continue buying land, conducting scientific experiments, and supporting his family. James abused William's good nature, albeit unwittingly, and left William responsible for his many debts. Now, all of a sudden it seemed, William was without access to funds. At the same time, the wife of a close friend, after whom he and Lizzie had named their second son, died; in July another friend's son, a boy of fifteen, drowned. William took these deaths hard, and then, worst of all, William and Lizzie's sturdy six-year-old, Jamie, began bleeding from his sinuses. Doctors told the worried parents that Jamie was suffering from an incurable disease called *Purpurea Haemmoragica* (the hemorrhaging of subcutaneous capillaries) and that even if he got better, "the slightest physical effort would bring on the disease again."

William was a sensitive, impressionable man, probably prone to mood swings and occasional bouts of depression. His investments had become worthless, and he was heavily in debt. His association with the American Institute at the Crystal Palace had disintegrated with it in flames. Two of his friends were in mourning, and his little boy seemed very ill. On October 28, 1858, William had watched over his son all afternoon. Sometime before five o'clock, for reasons no one will ever be sure about, he walked out of the house and never came home again. His death was attributed to drowning and so listed in official records. Family members must have known what happened, but there was a deliberate silence about the tragedy. If there were letters, they were destroyed. Lizzie never once mentioned William's death to anyone. Whether this was pride, grief, or purposefulness, we will never know. But, as Catharine Morris Wright noted: ". . . this tragedy was the cornerstone of her life and only due to it did she bud and flourish as the world knew her."

Lizzie gathered up her boys, a few of William's books and his shaving stand, and the blue Spode china and returned to Mapleridge. Lonely and grieving, far from her friends and life and unprepared for heartache, Lizzie struggled. She had to earn a living in order to support her boys. Her father, loving as he was, couldn't help. Writing had been a pleasant task before; now it had become a necessity. So in order to repay the mountain of loans her father and husband had incurred, she set to work. In 1861 she became sole editor and author of all sections of *Working Farmer* except the agricultural ones. Not known for her feminism, Lizzie certainly was a believer in equality for men and women, for she wrote in her first issue as editor: "Depend upon it, your home will become happier and better regulated should the lady of the house have some independence of her own. On the first of January 1862 take the tightening gold and silver band from your wife's brain and bid her think for herself. It may be a risk, especially for those who have married dolls instead of women . . . this time risk something in the hope of becoming happier." Another article, written in 1862, was titled "How to Avoid a Bad Husband." Perhaps this came from her own marital experience, perhaps from watching a passive mother, perhaps from her father's strong encouragement of his daughter. In any case, it was the first professional effort of Lizzie's career.

Lizzie needed a place of her own to write and to raise her boys. Mapleridge was legally hers—William had left it to her with all its liens and mortgages. But even if she had wanted to, she would never have sold Mapleridge as long as her father was alive. She determined to move into the empty attic of a building behind the house. Calling it "The Den," Lizzie filled it with books, a desk, interesting pictures, and a big comfortable chair. It was certainly not fancy, with a carpet of rags and no curtains at the windows, but it soon became as full of life and friends as Mapleridge was for her father. Lizzie began to emerge from her cloud of grief. Mornings were spent writing; afternoons were spent with Jamie and Harry, swimming or skating or storytelling. She began writing for Harper's *New Monthly Magazine,* and they took whatever she sent. In 1864 Lizzie's first book, *Irvington Stories,* published by James O'Kane, appeared and sold well. Despite the ongoing tragedy of civil war, life at home was good again.

Lizzie had a contract for a second book to appear in 1865, and for a long time she had wanted to write a book about Holland. She tried out the idea on Jamie and Harry, who encouraged her to write the story and listened eagerly to the narrative as it unfolded every night. In order to broaden her knowledge about nineteenth-century Dutch life as well as the European pastime of skating, she turned to the Scharffs, an outgoing, active Newark family whose sons were friends of Jamie. They were indeed helpful, and in the preface of the book she called *Hans Brinker or, The Silver Skates*, she wrote, "I turn with especial gratitude to those kind Holland friends who, with generous zeal, have taken many a backward glance at their country for my sake . . ." At first Lizzie's publisher did not want the book, considering it an unappealing guidebook. Still, O'Kane did not want to lose the young author whose *Irvington Stories* had gone into five editions in the first year of its life and about which the *North American Review* had written: "Good books for children are so rare, and books to make little spoonies so common, that this should be praised." He gave in, and a year after the debut of *Irvington Stories*, Lizzie secured the copyright of *Hans Brinker*. No one could have guessed that it would become a bestseller, that she would earn the French Academy's Prix Montheyon for it, or that it would prove to be one of the most famous children's books of all time, published in more than a hundred editions and translated into a half dozen languages within thirty years. It was so popular, in fact, that many years later, when Lizzie's son entered a bookstore to ask for a good book on Dutch life while on an 1881 trip to Holland, the clerk recommended *Hans Brinker*, not realizing that his customer's mother was the American author!

Lizzie's beloved father died just weeks after the success of *Hans Brinker*, and she became the breadwinner and head of the family. Her mother and sisters took care of her children as she forged forward and was introduced into New York literary circles, cementing life-long friendships with Louisa May Alcott, Frances Hodgson Burnett, and Lucia Gilbert Calhoun Runkle, the first woman on the editorial staff of the *New York Times*. In 1868 Lizzie published her adult game book, *A Few Friends and How They Amused Themselves* and, more important, was offered the associate editorship, under Harriet Beecher Stowe and Donald G. Mitchell, of *Hearth and Home*. Jamie, now sixteen and a handful, was an extremely bright young man. He wanted to go off to college and ultimately chose brand-new Cornell University. Lizzie would have to pay for it, and it was expensive. She took the job, for $1,500 a year with hope of sharing in some profits, and loved it, producing articles on literary subjects, domestic concerns, and artistic and scientific endeavors. Remaining very involved in the lives of her boys, Lizzie was teacher, friend, and companion. In order to juggle the roles of breadwinner, writer, and mother, she commuted daily between Waverly and New York, balancing heavy writing and editorial responsibilities with the obligations of a parent.

In 1873 Lizzie—with hundreds of stories, articles, and verses written and with an international reputation as a juvenile author—was approached by *Scribner's Monthly*, a superior-quality magazine for adults, to be the editor for a new children's publication that was to have the highest excellence in both literary content and presentation. Would she accept the position? This was a difficult decision for her. She was now an established writer and wanted to pursue that career. But, still mired down fifteen years later with William's mortgages and unpaid loans, Lizzie needed the $5,000 a year the position offered. Furthermore, she felt strongly that children's literature was sadly lacking. Magazines for children had been in vogue since the early 1800s, both in England and the United States. They usually set out to provide examples of good behavior for children but often ended up being too moralistic or, at worst, frightening. Child protagonists were often punished for minor infractions and, as Lizzie had noted, some of this output was not only dull but also harmful to children.

To counteract the void in good stories for children, Lizzie created adventures in serial form as part of every day's play with Jamie and Harry. "Many gifted men and women were writing novels; no one was doing all that could be done—ought to be done—for the boys and girls," she said. Determined to create literature that was strong, true, bold, fresh, joyous, and uncompromising, Lizzie took the job as editor.

Now the magazine needed a name. Such was Charles Scribner's faith in Lizzie that he left it to her to name the new publication, saying: "It is your magazine; do what you think best." Lizzie named it after the children's saint, St. Nicholas. Her publication would provide gifts of fun and learning. It would delight children as well as give them a voice. There would be no sermonizing, no talking down, no moralistic lessons except those naturally contained in the good stories themselves. Under Lizzie's capable hand, the first issue of *St. Nicholas* was printed and distributed in 1873.

Would it be a success? A publisher had to be optimistic to launch a young people's magazine in 1873. The American economy was in a depression, and many children's publications had recently failed. Regardless, *Scribner's Monthly* put the full weight of its finances and editorial staff behind *St. Nicholas* and sent it unhesitatingly into the world.

Children loved *St. Nicholas* immediately. Young readers said, "The day on which *St. Nicholas* arrived was like a holiday." Lizzie's ideas about what a magazine for children should contain were brilliant. There was the serialized fiction that kept young subscribers waiting with bated breath month after month. There were poems, articles, wonderful illustrations, and reproductions of fine paintings and photos. Lizzie insisted that the art should stand on its own, saying, "One of the sins of this age is editorial dribbling over inane pictures." She also believed that children should be told the truth: "Harsh, cruel facts—if they must come and sometimes it is important that they should—must march forward boldly, say what they have to say, and go," she said. It was because of Lizzie's innovative ideas and intuitive understanding of children's hearts and minds that *St. Nicholas* became the standard by which all succeeding children's magazines have been judged.

Lizzie had a nine-point plan for *St. Nicholas,* and this goal was met in every issue: Provide fun, stimulate the imagination and an appreciation of art, instill respect for country and family, offer insights into the world at large, provide positive ideals and role models, and offer the best literary work available. With such authors as Mark Twain and Laura Ingalls Wilder and such illustrators as M. C. Wyeth and Arthur Rackham, the achievement of Lizzie's goals was assured.

Ably supported by her assistant editor, Frank R. Stockton, Lizzie also contributed extensive articles and jingles to *St. Nicholas,* writing under the pen name Joel Stacy. Surprisingly she was never listed as editor in the publication. Rather, the cover page read: *St. Nicholas: An Illustrated Magazine For Young Folks* "conducted" by Mary Mapes Dodge. Indeed, she was a conductor, keeping the magazine on the right track, seeking fine literary creations from her contributors, and producing a body of work whose leitmotiv was a harmonious concert of spirited, memorable achievements.

Because Lizzie was widely known in literary circles, she had no trouble reaching out to the finest writers of the day for material. She pursued her colleagues with single-minded stubbornness as well as carefully reading manuscripts from such "unknowns" as Edna St. Vincent Millay and Rudyard Kipling and publishing them for the first time in the magazine. As *St. Nicholas* became established as a fine forum for writers, they clamored to appear in its pages. So it was that the likes of Sidney Lanier, John Greenleaf Whittier, Louisa May Alcott, Henry Wadsworth Longfellow, Frances Hodgson Burnett, Stephen Vincent Benet, Faith Baldwin, Ring Lardner, Emily Dickinson, Eugene Field, Christina Rossetti, Robert Louis Stevenson, Alfred Lord Tennyson, Cornelia Otis Skinner, James Russell Lowell, Charles Dickens, Helen Hunt Jackson, and Rebecca Harding Davis appeared regularly in *St. Nicholas*'s pages.

Lizzie wrote for and edited the ongoing departments in *St. Nicholas*, including "Jack-in-the-Pulpit," "The Riddle Box" (with rebuses, acrostics, and word puzzles contributed by children that might be impossible for adults to solve today), and "The Letter Box," a feature of every issue. On these pages children (and sometimes grown-ups) from all over the world poured out their hearts to *St. Nicholas*. "I suppose I must be called one of the big ones as I am eighteen: But I am just as fond of you as when I was eight," wrote Molly from Blackstone, England. "I live up in the Rocky Mountains . . . I have two sisters and a brother. . . . We all enjoy your stories very much," wrote Annie from Boulder Valley, Montana. "Our mails from San Francisco come twice a month, and sometimes we have to wait for the papers," wrote Clarence from Honolulu, Hawaiian Islands, in 1888. "I think it is very good of you to publish letters from little girls and boys. Reading these letters made me want to write, too. . . ."

Perhaps the favorite part of the magazine was the "St. Nicholas League," formed as an outlet for children's own creativity, a place to which they could contribute original fiction, art, photographs, and poetry. Gold and silver buttons were awarded as first and second prizes by the League; if you won those, you became entitled to win cash prizes. Of course the greatest glory for a young author was to see his or her work in print. For some contributors, it was the very beginning of life as a writer. Such notable authors as Stephen Vincent Benet, Rachel Field, and Faith Baldwin, among many others, first saw their work in print in *St. Nicholas.*

St. Nicholas so far surpassed any other children's magazine on the market that four other magazines were absorbed into it within the first few years of Lizzie's editorship—*Our Young Folks, The Children's Hour, The Schoolday Magazine,* and *The Little Corporal.* Later, *Wide Awake* magazine of Boston also merged with *St. Nicholas.*

Lizzie did not completely ignore her own writing. *Rhymes and Jingles* was published in 1874 and was followed in 1877 by *Theophilus and Others,* a collection of stories, sketches, and essays. In 1879 her adult collection of poems appeared as *Along the Way.* She continued with *Donald and Dorothy,* which first appeared as a serial in *St. Nicholas, The Land of Pluck,* and *When Life is Young,* a collection of verses.

Lizzie, forty-two when she began her editorship of *St. Nicholas,* became a stout, white-haired, poker-playing grandmother as the years went by. She was at the center of a distinguished group of writers, artists, and other creative types at her New York apartment, in Newark, and at her beloved summer cottage, purchased in 1888, in Onteora Park in the Catskills. She called it "Yarrow" after the wildflowers that grew around its doors, and over the fireplace was inscribed Wordsworth's lines: "Enough if in our hearts we know / There's such a place as Yarrow."

But all was not well. Lizzie wrote to her sister Kate in 1880:

"This past year has been the hardest of my life. I have not been well . . . Then Jamie's marriage and going away from us (which was a trial however we might love Josie [Jamie's wife]). Then Harry's weak eyes and the terrible Typhoid. Then a siege of Estate troubles—all brought about by my signing papers for Father's & Charley's old business matters when I was a young widow and which resulted in the total loss of my Waverly house and property and a judgement against me for many thousand dollars: then Harry's terrible second illness . . . the summer finds me rather worn and feeble . . . I figure my actual losses through sickness, business affairs and estate matters during the past few years at nearly $9,500."

Harry was a troubled boy. He suffered from anxiety and depression and had problems making his way in the world. He was alternately extremely attentive and then distant from his strong mother. A severe case of typhoid exacerbated his "nervousness," and Lizzie's presence seemed to make him worse. She must have seen his father in him. On February 2, 1881, Harry died suddenly of what was then called "congestion of the brain." He was twenty-six. Lizzie was resolute and strong and practical and, as always, when bludgeoned by life, quickly resumed its predictable patterns. But from her new apartment at Fifty-first Street and Broadway in New York, she wrote to Kate: "I am feeling as well & strong as one possibly could expect—But, oh Kate you know how it must be to me [Lizzie's sister Kate had lost a daughter] . . . I have no son with me now, in my daily life. I am so blessed & happy in Harry's beautiful life & noble character—and in the dear ones still left that I must not complain . . . I must try to be happy alone . . . I long for their fresh young companionship that was so precious to me in the years that went so soon. We were like a sister & her brothers in those day [sic]—and it still could be so if we were together."

With a continuing strong helm at *St. Nicholas* and at the eye of a creative hurricane of writers and artists, Lizzie edited, traveled, and held court in the Catskills. In 1903 the *Newark News* ran a sketch of their favored citizen. Covered were Lizzie's father, Professor Mapes, and his experimental pear trees and his charming wife, Sophia. Yet, oddly, the articles left out the core of Lizzie's life—William's disappearance and the debts, nor did they mention "two little boys, with big eyes, waiting at their mother's garret door until she finished writing and let them in."

Lizzie was busy and happy. Scribner's brought out a new edition of her poems for children that summer, and the Century Co. issued a new copy of her poems and verse in early fall. *St. Nicholas* thrived, although her editorial involvement had lessened in the previous few years, and Lizzie's grandchild was married in 1905. But her excursion to the wedding would be her last. She had begun to fall seriously ill with recurring severe pain in her stomach, loss of appetite, and jaundice. The doctors diagnosed her with gall bladder disease, but Lizzie had cancer. She died on August 21, 1905, at Onteora. At the services her poem "The Two Mysteries" was read. The children of Onteora carried a great cross of yarrow for which they had gathered the blooms. The next day this cross was laid on her grave in Evergreen Cemetery, next to her father and mother, sisters Louise and Sophie, and her darling boy, Harry. Far away in Brooklyn, William lay alone.

In spite of her troubles, Lizzie had remained "that live spark of a woman." Her brother had said of her, "Lizzie deserves it all and more if possible for she has bravely fought her battle and kept her courage when the present was not pleasant and the future far from promising. Lizzie is a trump—and no wonder she has won the hearts of thousands of youngsters."

Many readers say that *St. Nicholas* began to decline after Lizzie's death, when her fine hand and heart could no longer lead. Others say it only began its decline after the 1920s. Regardless, *St. Nicholas* continued until February 1940, when it ceased publication. It is still extraordinary to read today, full of wonderful fiction, informative nonfiction, lovely poetry, and compelling art. It also, despite the vow of St. Nicholas League members to protect the oppressed, reflects the prejudices of its time. A poem entitled "Imitation Japanese" described the Japanese mother as having "beady eyes and a funny name"; an article called "Novel Christmas Presents" parodied a black maid with the lines, "I am de jolly waiter-gal / Who rings de bell for tea. / I'se brought you here a plate ob jam / As nice as nice can be!," and Africans "discovered" by Stanley Livingston were described as childish savages. However, although it did fall prey to assumptions of the day, *St. Nicholas* also endeavored to bring information about faraway cultures to children and to do it as kindly as possible within its stated goal of being unwilling to see others deprived of life and liberty.

Lizzie had good reason to be proud. She set up a model for children's literature that has never been bested. Her editorial leadership and high standards created a magical, educational, and joyful world for children. She made the world around her better with her infectious gaiety and her kind goodwill. Her warmth was legendary, her bravery undeniable. Still, her best memorial remains the love of millions of children whose lives were gladdened and minds opened by her stories, her poems, and her radiant editorship of *St. Nicholas*. "Through all her laurelled years of triumph and success," wrote William Fayal Clarke in a memorial to Lizzie in the October 1905 issue of *St. Nicholas*, "her heart was as the heart of a little child."

CLARA MAASS

1876–1901

Yellow Fever Nurse

"*G*oodbye, Mother. Don't worry. God will care for me in the yellow fever hospital the same as if I were at home. I will send you nearly all I earn, so be good to yourself and the two little ones. You know I am the man of the family, but do pray for me."

These final words came from the pen of twenty-five-year-old Clara Maass as she lay dying in far-off Havana, Cuba—her body tortured with high fever, intense joint and muscle pain, and blinding headaches. Her concern for her widowed mother and siblings at home in New Jersey was uppermost in her mind, though, and despite her torment, she made this last attempt to bid them farewell.

It was 1901. The brief Spanish-American War was over. Actual combat had resulted in only 968 deaths. But there was another war that was still being fought—one that had claimed the lives of more than 5,000 soldiers during the course of military action in Cuba and would continue to strike down occupying forces in army camps in staggering numbers. The real enemy was yellow fever—a disease that was pervasive, vicious, and deadly.

Clara, a contract nurse on special assignment at Las Animas Hospital in Havana, had volunteered to be bitten by a mosquito in

Clara Maass

an experiment that was intended both to confirm the connection between mosquito bites and yellow fever and to prove that lifetime immunity could be attained by risking a mild case of the disease in controlled medical surroundings. Volunteers were solicited for this highly dangerous endeavor and were promised $100 for their participation—money Clara needed to send home to her mother, who struggled daily to feed and clothe Clara's brothers and sisters.

On June 24, 1901, Clara had allowed herself to be bitten by a mosquito thought to be infected with yellow fever. She contracted a mild case of the disease and recovered quickly. But doctors doubted that the slight case she had contracted had immunized her.

The season moved into the sultry days of August. The heavy tropical air was thick with mosquitoes seeking new hosts. Clara volunteered yet again. On August 14 she watched as a fully infected mosquito punctured her arm. This time there was no question. Clara had contracted a severe case of yellow fever and soon became deathly ill. Her temperature soared; headaches caused her to writhe in agony. On August 24 she died, but not in vain.

The guilt of the mosquito had been proven beyond a shadow of a doubt. It was not close quarters or contaminated clothing or dirty conditions that caused yellow fever but the simple bite of an insect. Experiments on human victims could now end and the work of eradicating the disease could begin. *The New York Times* editorialized in Clara's obituary, "No soldier in the late war placed his life in peril for better reasons than those which prompted this faithful nurse to risk hers." And the Committee on Pensions wrote this official epitaph for the brave Clara: "From this point of view the death of Miss Maass greatly contributed to establishing the fact that yellow fever was conveyed by the mosquito."

Clara Louise Maass was born on June 28, 1876, in East Orange, New Jersey, the oldest of nine children. Her parents,

Robert and Hedwig, were German immigrants, part of a large influx of Germans who since 1848 had filled the neighborhood of Germantown in West Newark. Indeed, by 1865, nearly one-third of Newark's 100,000 residents were of German heritage. Though some immigrants found success, most struggled as factory workers. According to Robert D. B. Carlisle's *Building Bridges for 125 Years,* ". . . yeast clouds from the breweries, mingled with the rising odor of filth that spattered the rough streets . . ." hardly kept European immigrants from "squeezing into any rooming house or small dwelling they could find." Employers used these newcomers to turn out leather goods, hats, paints, luggage, and celluloid, among other products, in the sprawling industrial city. Cholera, malaria, and typhoid were frequent visitors to tenement housing. By Clara's fourteenth year, the city's death rate was higher than it had been before the Civil War. Men at this time, including Clara's father, a hatter who worked seasonally for low pay, had a life expectancy of less than forty-one years. Her mother struggled to manage their children on so miserly an income, and Clara, being the oldest, carried the lion's share of burdens. She was a substitute mother, nurse, and housekeeper and knew only endless days of grinding work. Although Clara's birth had been greeted with joy, by the time she was in grade school there was barely enough food to feed all the Maass children. Clara was sent to live with another family as a hired girl. There she cleaned house and took care of the children for board, room, and time off to go to school. She was not paid. This may seem cruel, but among the working poor in the nineteenth century, it was not unusual for large families to farm out older children, both to relieve demands at home and to ensure food and a place to sleep for the eldest.

When Clara was around twelve, her family moved to a farm in Livingston. There she experienced a real childhood for the first time in her life: regular schooling, play in the country, and some time to herself. Unfortunately her family's efforts at farming failed; Clara returned with them to East Orange and went back to work as a hired girl.

In spite of never-ending labor, Clara completed three years at East Orange High School before she was forced to leave school at fifteen to work full time. Her first job was at the Newark Orphan Asylum, where she received $10 a month for feeding, dressing, and caring for the children seven days a week. She split this money with her family.

This was torment for the intelligent, ambitious girl who wanted nothing more than to learn. How much she must have wanted to finish high school! There was never a hint of resentment from Clara, though, who was said to have a charming personality; she either hid her disappointments well or transformed her regrets into a desire to serve. In those days there were few acceptable ways women could express their intelligence and energy. Service to the community was one, and independent Clara could at least find self-satisfaction knowing her contributions were irreplaceable.

Newark's thriving German population had a strong need for adequate medical care, both for treatment of disease and for victims of increasingly common industrial accidents. After a series of difficulties with the city at large over creating a new general hospital, the German community banded together to create its own. The Newark German Hospital opened on December 27, 1870, and, although the hospital was created and operated by the German community, it offered services to patients of every nationality and status.

The hospital saw many firsts, not only within the local area but also within the country. Here was the site of the city's first cesarean section and the country's first successful bowel resection. Doctors instituted an antiseptic environment in the operating room—not exactly the norm at the time—and a health insurance plan was developed for interested groups to help defray medical expenses. In addition, an active women's auxiliary raised impressive amounts of money for hospital projects such as buying basic supplies and equipping the hospital with beds and linens.

Still, Newark German Hospital desperately needed good nurses in order to end its reliance on the services of untrained housecleaners or orderlies, and the hospital's physicians wanted women educated in caring for the sick. Soon a rigorous nursing program that included instruction, training, and internship was developed. Christina Trefz, wife of a local brewery magnate, felt that nurses in training needed a real school of their own. Though not a nurse, Trefz had observed the nurses' need for dormitories and lecture halls. With astounding speed and generosity, Trefz bought some vacant lots adjacent to the hospital and had a building constructed. On November 30, 1893, Trefz Hall, a Training School for Nurses, was dedicated. It had a lecture room, bedrooms for fourteen students, baths (at a time when most families still had outdoor privies), and a living room for socializing. The hospital advertised for candidates between the ages of twenty and forty, "of good character and with proof of physical ability." Potential students were also required to have a general education and some command of English.

Nursing school offered seventeen-year-old Clara a previously undreamed-of opportunity—to receive advanced education and to be provided with room and board and $5.00 a month. The only entrance requirement of the new school was approval by Anna Seeber, the uncompromising head nurse and director of the nursing school.

Clara responded to the ads, even though she was three years short of the youngest age requirement. Seeber immediately took to Clara, no doubt appreciating her maturity, no-frills appearance, experience, and history of hard work. It also didn't hurt that Clara spoke both German and English, for most of her lessons and instructions from doctors, patients, and the head nurse would come in German. Clara passed her entrance exam—acceptance by Seeber—and was admitted to nursing school.

It was an exhausting two years of lectures, hours on the floor and in operating and birthing rooms, as well as in wards where people died daily of disease. However, Clara was used to long hours and hard work and became popular with her colleagues and her patients. On October 12, 1895, she and three other graduates received their diplomas and black-bordered caps. Clara stayed on at the hospital, adding to her small wages by taking on private nursing jobs. She must have been a truly inspired healer. History shows that she was held in high esteem by the medical staff, for in 1898 she was named head nurse of Newark German Hospital at the tender age of twenty-one.

While Clara nursed the sick in New Jersey, great events were playing out on the world's stage. As a result of America's rapid economic, territorial, and cultural expansion during the 1890s, the United States had become embroiled in the Spanish-American War and subsequent occupation of Cuba. Many white Americans felt morally obligated to spread their traditions in faraway places, just as colonialist British, French, and Germans had done in Asia and Africa. This "territorial imperative" was whipped into a frenzy by the "yellow" journalistic practices of Joseph Pulitzer of the *New York World* and William Randolph Hearst of the *New York Journal*, who printed exaggerated reports of Spanish atrocities against Cuban revolutionaries in order to sell newspapers. All reached a head when the battleship *Maine* exploded in Havana harbor in January 1898. No one knows who or what caused the explosion, but Hearst's cry of "Remember the Maine, to hell with Spain" created a jingoistic fever of support for American intervention. On April 25, 1898, Congress declared war on Spain.

The war was brief, but it was long enough for thousands of

soldiers to be stricken by malaria, typhoid, and, the greatest killer of all, yellow fever when they traveled to Spanish-owned Cuba and other tropical areas. The Army feared sending these soldiers home, lest they contaminate the civilian population.

Yellow fever, so called because the sufferer turns a yellowish color due to liver damage, had been the scourge of tropical and sub-tropical areas of the world for centuries. During warm seasons it had stretched its infectious tentacles into temperate areas of the United States. There were continuous and severe outbreaks in Florida and New Orleans, earning that city the title of "yellow fever capital of the United States." New York was hit by an outbreak as early as 1668, Philadelphia in the 1790s, and Memphis in 1879.

Yellow fever begins suddenly after an incubation period of three to five days, with fever, chills, internal bleeding, rapid heart-beat, severe headache, back pains, and extreme weakness. Jaundice usually appears on the second or third day. In the final stages, inter-nal hemorrhaging leads to projectile vomiting of blood, followed by delirium and coma and eventually death. Yellow fever was terri-fying because it began with fairly innocuous flu symptoms yet killed so quickly. Its mortality rate often reached 85 percent, and no one had any idea how it was spread or how to stop it.

American politicians and military leaders demanded a solu-tion to the problem of yellow fever. Fifty thousand American sol-diers were stationed in Cuba as part of an occupation army, and all were vulnerable to the terrible disease. Surgeon General of the Army George Miller Sternberg and Governor General of Cuba Leonard Wood assigned Major William Crawford Gorgas and his sanitation officers to clean up American camps and the streets of Havana. They were convinced that sanitary measures would eradi-cate the disease. They were wrong. By mid-July yellow fever was rampant. Frustrated, Sternberg and Wood appointed a team of Army research scientists to study the causes of the disease in Cuba.

They selected four men to the commission, with Major Walter Reed as director.

Almost twenty years previously, Havana physician Dr. Carlos Finlay had stated that mosquitos were the carriers of yellow fever. American researchers dismissed the theory, calling it ridiculous, although Walter Reed wanted to reexamine its feasibility. Reed, along with his staff—James Carroll, Aristides Agramonte, and Jesse Lazear—set to work. Lazear was accidentally bitten during the experiments and died of yellow fever.

Clara Maass was quite aware of the situation in Cuba. She had wanted to enlist, but nurses were not allowed to do so. So she applied to be a contract nurse. In the early fall of 1898, Clara was accepted and sent to the field hospital of the Seventh U.S. Army Corps at Jacksonville, Florida. Hundreds of soldiers were sick and dying from malaria, typhoid fever, and dysentery. Clara had much experience with typhoid fever in particular, having treated it regularly at Newark German Hospital. She worked all day, sleeping in a tent at night with three other nurses. Eventually she was transferred to Savannah, then, briefly, to Santiago de Cuba, where she nursed her first yellow fever patient. She was released from her Army contract in February 1899. In November of the same year, Clara wrote to the Surgeon General, asking for an assignment to Manila, where U.S. troops had been stationed in response to an insurrection in the Philippines. In the letter Clara wrote that she preferred a tropical climate to that of New York and that she was "in excellent health" with "a good constitution" and "accustomed to the hardships of field service."

Clara nursed in Manila for seven months, working tirelessly to bring comfort to men sick and dying from typhoid and malaria as well as yellow fever. When she was struck down with dengue, called "breakbone fever" because of the agonizing pain it caused in the joints and muscles, her slow recovery forced the Army to send her home to recuperate.

Meanwhile in Cuba, Gorgas, still skeptical of the mosquito theory, sought to prove that a clean, sanitary environment would stem yellow fever outbreaks, and he needed nurses to treat and care for patients in such an environment.

Clara had a lot to live for when she responded to Gorgas's call for nurses to attend patients in Havana in the fall of 1900. She was planning marriage to a New York businessman. But to Clara, duty always came first. On October 14 Gorgas telegraphed Clara with the plea to "come at once," and she left for Cuba and the civilian Las Animas Hospital with all due speed. It was there that Dr. John Guiteras shared with her the plan to conduct human experiments. Although not officially sponsored by Reed's Army team, such experiments were watched with careful interest by all concerned. But Clara was discouraged from participating in human testing, no doubt because she was a woman as well as a valued nurse.

In late spring 1901, volunteers were offered $100 by the Army to participate in an experiment that consisted of being bitten by the *Stegomyia* mosquito and, hopefully, contracting a case of yellow fever that was mild enough to be controlled by keeping patients under close medical care but strong enough to provide lifetime immunity. Although dismayed by the recent deaths of two experimental subjects, Clara volunteered. She hoped that the $100 would pay off some of her mother's debts and would also provide funds to bring her sister to Cuba to be with her and eventually take her place after she returned to New Jersey to get married. Clara hoped to continue her nursing work after her marriage, so the subsequent immunity she would possess would help her to more effectively care for afflicted patients without the worry of being stricken herself.

In June Clara submitted to the first experiment, resulting in a mild case of yellow fever—too mild, it was thought, to render her immune to the disease. So on August 14 Clara gave her arm to the mosquito again, this time fatally. She was the last human experiment victim to die. She was also the only nurse to die, the only woman to die, and the only American of the nineteen volunteers to die.

Mostly due to Clara's death, the outcry against human testing reached a crescendo. But by this time, the true cause of yellow fever had been identified and plans already set in motion to wipe out the mosquito population from Cuba and other tropical areas. Eventually a vaccine was developed to further protect against a yellow fever outbreak. Future generations would be protected from the disease.

Clara was immediately buried in Havana, but in 1902 her coffin was returned to New Jersey for interment with military honors in Fairmount Cemetery in Newark. Her mother received an Army pension to help with the expenses that had weighed so heavily on Clara's mind. Pensions to civilians were rare, but Clara's services were deemed to have been "of a military character at the time of her death."

Clara's noble actions were eulogized both in spoken and printed word for a while, but new issues and concerns soon took center stage. For many years it seemed as though Clara had been forgotten by all but family members and friends.

More than twenty-five years had passed when another employee of Newark Memorial (formerly German) Hospital inspired a renewed interest in Clara and her life. Leopoldine Guinther, a superintendent of nursing, read a commemorative anniversary story about Clara. Touched by the story, she eventually raised enough money to install a new headstone at Clara's neglected gravesite. Made of pink Milford granite and bronze, the headstone bears a likeness of Clara and a brief account of the yellow fever experiment. The epitaph reads, "Greater love hath no man [sic] than this." In 1949 Newark Memorial Hospital (now called Lutheran Memorial) initiated two Clara Maass Scholarships for Cuban girls who want to study professional nursing at the hospital. Upsala College named a new dormitory Clara Maass Hall in 1950, and Las Animas Hospital dedicated a pavilion in her honor. Cuba issued a stamp in tribute to Clara, as did the U.S. Postal Service during the bicentennial. And in 1952 the giant Lutheran Memorial Hospital was renamed Clara Maass Memorial Hospital. These honors pale next to the real legacy of Clara's sacrifice—a world free of the scourge of yellow fever.

JESSIE REDMON FAUSET

1882–1961

Midwife of the
Harlem Renaissance

*J*essie sat silently, listening to her teacher. Her face appeared calm, her body quiet. But inside her roiled a sea of emotions; she felt so alone. When she had entered the doors of the prestigious Philadelphia High School for Girls that morning, she had felt proud and excited. Now, close to tears, she understood that all the fine manners she'd been taught, the elegance of her upbringing, mattered little. She was colored in a white world, and nobody, not even her best friends, would ever forget it. What agony. The girls with whom she had played and studied in her grammar-school days looked away when she spoke to them. Her heart was full of tears, but she sat stolid and resolute. No matter her hurt and anger, she would learn, she would endure—she would prevail.

Jessie Redmon Fauset was born on April 27, 1882, in Fredericksville, a small town in Camden County. She was the seventh child and fifth daughter of Anna Seamon and Redmon Fauset. Her family history was a source of great personal pride. Unlike most other blacks, the Fausets had been free for several generations. They were

Jessie Redmon Fauset

urban and Northern, and they were relatively privileged, although the community itself was poor. Jessie's father was pastor at the Mt. Pisgah African Methodist Episcopal Church in the all-black settlement of Snow Hill. The Mt. Pisgah church was a significant focal point in local African-American life and culture. Also known as Free Haven, her community had been founded by Quakers to provide refuge for escaped slaves. However, because the Fausets moved to Philadelphia when Jessie was young, she missed the opportunity to grow up in an all-black environment where she might have been nurtured as a woman of color. Instead she grew up in a white neighborhood, where the scars of racism left lasting marks on her psyche.

That injury was further amplified by the early death of her mother and four of her siblings. (Redmon Fauset remarried a woman named Belle Huff. Belle had three children of her own, and she and Redmon would have three more children together.) This intensified the bond between Jessie and her father and sister Helen. Redmon Fauset was almost fifty when Jessie was born. She adored and idolized him, attributed her writing talent to him, and adopted his ideals of service and upward-striving her entire life. But she also felt honor bound to adopt his ethical and conservative values, and this would always be a source of internal conflict for her, especially in her literary endeavors. For Redmon Fauset's daughter, respectability was everything, as was seriousness of purpose and conservatism of demeanor. Methodist teachings placed many restrictions on the young, impressionable girl. "I might not sing songs, I might not play, I didn't know how to write letters, it was wrong to read even fairy-tales," wrote Jessie about Sunday afternoon.

As with many other upwardly mobile blacks, Jessie's father prized education—reading and an active examination of religion, politics, and pertinent race issues—above all else. Jessie exceeded his expectations. Raised to be a teacher, she won admission to the academically competitive Philadelphia High School for Girls and did superior work. Jessie felt "agony" on her entrance day there when, as the only black girl at school, she was totally ignored by white girls with whom she had played as a child; they "refused to acknowledge my greeting." Jessie rose above the snubs and cruelty to prosper and become an honor student, but upon graduation she was denied admission to any local colleges, as well as Bryn Mawr, because of her color. Bitter but not bowed, Jessie persevered until she won admission to Cornell University. At Cornell, Jessie studied four years of Latin, German, and English, along with two years of Greek and French as well as psychology, logic, ethics, archeology, and political science. She was elected to Phi Beta Kappa in 1905. Since records were not kept at the time, it is not known whether Jessie was the first black woman to achieve this honor, but it is quite likely she was. One thing is for certain: Jessie was the only black woman in a college community of more than 3,000 students and probably the first black woman to matriculate at Cornell. And by the time she graduated, she was certainly one of the best-educated African-Americans of her generation.

Still, Jessie realized that a huge chunk of her education was missing. While still at Cornell, she was put in touch with W. E. B. DuBois through one of her professors in order that she might increase her knowledge of her people's history. In 1903 she wrote to DuBois, author of the classic work *The Souls of Black Folk* and a professor at Atlanta University, asking that he help her acquire summer employment. "I want to work in the South," she wrote DuBois. "I know only one class of my people well, and I want to become acquainted with the rest." With DuBois's help, she succeeded in gaining an English-teaching position at Fisk University the next year, a job for which she was grateful and in which she felt useful. Jessie considered this teaching experience an important one in preparing for her future. It not only helped her to improve her skills before graduation from college but also afforded her the opportunity to become acquainted with blacks who had a different environment and upbringing from her own.

DuBois was teacher, mentor, and friend to Jessie, but he certainly became more when her father died in 1903. In many ways he took Redmon Fauset's place as critic and inspiration. He also encouraged her thoughts on racial pride as an essential component for progress and her belief that specific values and ideals transcended race.

When Jessie graduated from Cornell and sought a job teaching in Philadelphia high schools, she was rejected because of her race, even though these schools were integrated. Smarting, she went instead to Douglass High School in Baltimore and then to M Street High School in Washington, D.C., both segregated. She taught Latin and French for more than ten years, using part of her salary to help pay for her sister Helen's schooling.

The M Street High School (renamed in 1916 for poet Paul Laurence Dunbar) was the crown of black public secondary schools. Principal Anna Julia Cooper had developed the curriculum of the school into a college preparatory program—winning out over a congressional proposal to make the school a center for the industrial training of blacks. This elite institution trained the children of Washington's sizable black middle class and sent many of its graduates into the most prestigious universities in the country. In 1921, when the first three black women in the United States to earn doctorates received their degrees, two were on the staff of Dunbar High School.

The experience of living in a strictly segregated city strengthened Jessie's identification with the black political struggle. There were many intellectual outlets as well. She was close friends and colleagues with poet and playwright Angelina Grimke and finally met her hero, DuBois. During their correspondence, the National Association for the Advancement of Colored People (NAACP) was organized in 1910—an outgrowth of the Niagara Movement, a conference on civil liberties organized by DuBois and others. The NAACP was critical to the improvement of race relations, the elevation of the status of women, and the recognition of black intellectual and cultural achievements. Jessie was attracted to the organization, its goals, and its activities and became more actively involved. In 1912 she began contributing columns as well as articles, short fiction, personal essays, and poetry to DuBois's new journal and the NAACP's official publication, *The Crisis: A Record of the Darker Races,* founded in 1910 and ultimately gaining a readership of more than 95,000 subscribers. The journal set intellectual standards for a new generation of blacks.

In a further effort to broaden her experience and education, Jessie traveled to France in 1914 to study at the Sorbonne. On a sabbatical in 1918–19, she completed work for her master of arts degree in Romance languages at the University of Pennsylvania. Sometime during this period Jessie decided to leave teaching and become a writer. In 1918 she formalized her contract with *The Crisis,* agreeing to write a regular column called "The Looking Glass" at a salary of $50 a month. When idealistic, independent Jessie arrived in New York at the age of thirty-seven to assume the position of literary editor, her salary doubled to $100 a month.

The Crisis had by this time developed into a powerful presence in black intellectual and political life. Its aim was to report on matters of race and to assert the dangers of racism toward blacks in the United States. It published a small number of original articles and reviewed books and other works written on the "race problem." Readers of *The Crisis* were loyal, and they were heartened and uplifted by DuBois's support of "black folk," his passionate denunciation of racism, his proselytizing for Pan-Africanism, and his persistent honoring of black achievements. Though independent of the NAACP, it was asserted that without *The Crisis,* "there would be no Association," as *The Crisis* was the NAACP's primary tool for recruiting members. Further, it is impossible to overstate the importance of *The Crisis* in readers' lives. It was respected, revered, loved, and treasured. Some who could not afford the subscription price enclosed coins in envelopes, promising to send more later in order not to miss an issue.

Jessie was very happy to join *The Crisis* and arrived at an auspicious time. The war in Europe was over. Africa was soon to be liberated, it was believed, and everywhere people's hopes for a worldwide renaissance of harmony were expressed in the arts. In *The Crisis*, DuBois pointed out that while all Europe "rejoices in its new gifts *our* men, who have helped mightily to awaken and preserve the spirit which makes these things possible, are returning to what?"

Jessie's arrival also coincided with the first stirrings of what was soon called the Harlem Renaissance. It is no accident that the Harlem Renaissance occurred when it did. Beginning in the wake of The War to End All Wars, it thrived during freewheeling Prohibition and died with the Depression. It was shaped by new urbanization, mostly by patterns of black emigration from the rural South to the urban North after the war, by the desire to break through traditional racial barriers that resurged after World War I, and by the desire to uplift the black experience through creative expression in all forms of the arts. The New Negro movement embraced literature and included race-building and race pride, image-building, jazz, progressive and socialist politics, political propaganda, the black folk tradition, musical and sexual freedom, self-revelation (in literature), and the pursuit of hedonism. It was primarily a literary and intellectual movement, and its members made up a pantheon of talented black writers: W. E. B. DuBois, Langston Hughes, Zora Neale Hurston, Countee Cullen, Jean Toomer, and Jessie herself, among many others.

Harlem itself was an approximate 2-square mile corridor in

upper Manhattan. As migration from the South intensified (away from the lynching of blacks and the rise of the Ku Klux Klan), Harlem became a mecca for middle-class blacks as well. Such organizations as the Masons, the Elks, churches, the National Urban League, black newspapers, and the YMCA all provided residents a structure within which to live. Black cabaret culture began in the mid-1910s with afternoon tea and ragtime music. These events eventually morphed into wild parties with plenty of free-flowing liquor. Along with the more conservative groups, such political organizations as Marcus Garvey's African Nationalist Movement, the Universal Negro Improvement Association, and the social African Blood Brotherhood also prospered.

Jessie was liked by everyone, even the more radical members of the movement. She was a woman who supported herself, made a marked impact upon the literary world, and was not afraid to discuss racial and feminist issues. White guests were rarely present at the apartment Jessie shared with her sister Helen, "unless they were distinguished white people, because Jessie Fauset did not feel like opening her home to mere sightseers or faddists momentarily in love with Negro life." "Harlemania" was separate from the literary contributions of the Renaissance. Those in the New Negro movement looked upon popular culture as a fad that could be destructive to the raising up of black culture they were trying to achieve. Poetry, painting, and serious music were often valued over dancing, blues, and jazz; many black intellectuals also disapproved of the drugs, alcohol, and sex that came with the latter, although many—especially gay and lesbian and transgendered writers and musicians—participated fully in the underground life, where they were accepted without comment. Nevertheless, this was a time! Jessie stepped into it and ultimately became the mother of it as she "birthed" great poet after great poet into the world under the auspices of her editorship at *The Crisis*. Jessie would see to it that some of the best poetry of the period—that of Countee Cullen, Langston Hughes, Claude McKay, and Jean Toomer—appeared first under her keen and nurturing eye. Jessie took these new (some of high school age) writers under her wing, listened to them, counseled them, and provided them with a willing ear and supportive criticism as she introduced them to the world.

In addition to other issues, under Jessie's aegis as editor of *The Crisis*, the complex and particular subject of the black woman's plight was closely examined. The public had an image of black women, somewhat emphasized by a growing media influence, that was far from accurate and, at worst, simplistic. Jessie was determined to write about the conflicts this situation imposed upon black women and to define, literarily, the obstacles women needed to overcome in order to achieve a true sense of identity. She was also instrumental in publishing the work of black women in *The Crisis*, believing that the arts could help to meet and positively address gender issues that, for black women, were tied in a complicated web of prejudice and image.

Jessie also chose to expand the boundaries of her involvement within the Harlem Renaissance movement by penning lyrics for black singer, composer, and arranger Henry Thacker Burleigh, as well as becoming involved in the 1921 musical *Shuffle Along*. This all-black production has often been called the catalyst that paved the way for the Harlem Renaissance itself as well as for the emergence of African-American music in the 1920s.

The Crisis became the focus of Jessie's life. She took charge of all literary matters and acted as managing editor when DuBois was away. And all the time she honed her writing skills. During the 1920s many of her pieces—essays and articles, book reviews, translations, poetry, and short stories—appeared in *The Crisis*. In 1924 she published her first novel, *There Is Confusion*. Initially she experienced a great deal of resistance from publishers who believed that white readers would not be able to grasp the idea of a black middle class, a consistent theme in her novels, as well as her inter-weaving of class issues into the plot, both within and outside black culture. Ultimately *There Is Confusion* was published by the Boni and Liveright Company, whose stable of authors also included Faulkner, Dreiser, and Pound. This was followed during the next ten years by *Plum Bun,* a novel of racial passing; *The Chinaberry Tree,* which takes place in a small New Jersey town; and *Comedy: American Style,* which depicts the effects of self-hatred on a black woman and her family. Jessie's novels were often criticized for being too bour-geois in terms of the black experience. Some of this criticism grew from the contrast between Jessie's characters and the performers of the day, who presented an "earthier" image. Historians have posited that this contrast represents one of the many dilemmas of black women and the double challenge of race and gender, coupled with the stereotypical sexual image often assumed by the public to repre-sent all black women.

During this prolific time, Jessie was also one of the few black women to participate in the 1921 Pan-African Congress as well as to travel throughout Europe and the Middle East during 1925 and 1926. Traveling in France, Jessie found a freedom she could never have in the United States. "I like to live among people and sur-roundings where I am not always conscious of 'thou shall not,'" she told a reporter. "I am colored and wish to be known as colored . . . sometimes I have felt that my growth as a writer has been hampered in my own country." Jessie usually avoided her own compatriots abroad for that very reason. During this time Jessie translated and reviewed works by French-speaking black writers from Africa and the Caribbean. She never directly reported her own experiences at the 1921 congress, no doubt because the congress was primarily masculine centered. But a Scottish newspaper noted that Jessie had spoken "on the subject of black American women who had been a great force behind all the movements for emancipation in the U.S."

In 1920 and 1921 Jessie created a publication for children called *The Brownies' Book* (produced under the auspices of the NAACP), "designed for all children but especially for ours." In a poem in the first issue, Jessie wrote:

> To children who with eager look
> Scanned vainly library shelf and nook,
> For History or Song or Story
> That told of Colored Peoples' glory,—
> We dedicate The Brownies' Book.

The magazine printed short stories and poetry, African folk tales, puzzles, and monthly historical features. An amazing array of great figures was portrayed, including Harriet Tubman and Phillis Wheatley. Jessie also solicited manuscripts from wonderful writers who refused to "write down" to their readership and especially encouraged the participation of women writers and illustrators. *The Brownies' Book* ceased publication after only twenty-four issues, mainly because a subscription to a children's magazine was an impossible luxury for most black families. Nevertheless, while it lasted it offered black children something they had never had before—juvenile literature that looked and sounded like them.

In 1926, at the age of forty-five, Jessie decided to resign her post at *The Crisis.* Historians have speculated about her reasons for leaving. Some have suggested that Jessie was in love with her distinguished and brilliant editor. Others claim that Jessie was unhappy about DuBois's slowness in repaying a loan from her and Helen. Perhaps Jessie was just tired of working for DuBois, who was, by the majority of accounts, arrogant, difficult, irascible, and tiresome. Tellingly, while looking for a new position, she credited *The Crisis*, rather than its editor-in-chief, DuBois, as "the greatest single contributing factor in the growth of significant Negro writers." In doing so, she gave herself credit for her own brilliance and years of work. Jessie did not wish to return to teaching but had no other real career options. She had hoped to find a position as a publisher's reader or working for a foundation and had even offered "to work at home . . . if the question of color should come up." Her ambitions went nowhere, and in 1927 she returned to the classroom at DeWitt Clinton High School, where she taught until 1944 and wrote her last three novels during school vacations.

The stock market crash of October 29, 1929, ended the Harlem Renaissance. Quickly gone were dance clubs and black luminaries, replaced by breadlines, unemployment, and more subtle forms of racism. Harlem began the precipitous slide from ghetto to slum. "We were no longer in vogue . . . we Negroes," said Langston Hughes. "Colored actors began to go hungry, publishers politely rejected new manuscripts, and patrons found other uses for their money."

In 1929, at the age of forty-seven, Jessie married Herbert E. Harris, an official of the Victory Insurance Company, and moved to Montclair, New Jersey. An article in the *New York Amsterdam News* referred to Jessie's academic and literary accomplishments but paid special attention to her social status. After 1934 Jessie never published again, although she continued as a lecturer and teacher, offering such courses as "Negro Literature in America" at the adult school in Montclair, where she and her husband made their home at 245 Orange Road for two decades.

After her beloved sister Helen's death, Jessie funded a special section of books about black people, particularly children, for the public school where Helen had taught. Not only was this a touching tribute to her sister, but it also reemphasized the focus on education their parents had instilled in them so many years earlier. Jessie's husband died in 1958, and shortly thereafter Jessie moved to Philadelphia. Following a long bout with heart disease, Jessie died on April 30, 1961, at age seventy-nine.

Most critics and historians agree that Jessie was an essential and integral part of the Harlem Renaissance and that without her nurturance and promotion, those we recognize as geniuses today would never have received a reading, much less fame and a permanent place in the lexicon of great writers. Still, there remains severe disagreement as to her own skills as a writer and portrayer of the black experience.

In some cases critics accused her of selling out to the white world and savaged her work. No clearer example of this can be found than in the essay by Hiroko Sato entitled "Under the Harlem Shadow: A Study of Jessie Fauset and Nella Larsen." Sato says that Jessie "shows the tragic situation which faces many of the black intellectuals: They are making too much of the white world, so that they can never escape its influence." Sato felt that Jessie lacked as a writer and spokesperson for blacks, never having known "the life of the black people of the rural South, nor the ghettos of the Northern cities."

What choice did Jessie have? She had to write about the world she knew, and that world was the black middle class—refined, intellectual, and, except for color, not one whit different from the white one. Within this milieu, Jessie's point was that except for the biological accident of color, blacks were no different from whites and should be afforded the same privileges and opportunities as their white sisters and brothers. On closer examination, perhaps her mannered style was used to make her subjects, many of which were "hardly typical drawing room conversation topics in the mid 1920s," more palatable to her readers.

Most critics have not acknowledged Jessie's status as an early black feminist. Her novels' protagonists are all black women who struggle for equality in a society whose strictures prevent its attainment. It is sexism, along with racism, that her novels explore. "Fauset was a quiet rebel," writes Deborah E. McDowell in her essay "The Neglected Dimension of Jessie Redmon Fauset," "a pioneer black literary feminist, and . . . her characters were harbingers of the movement for women's liberation from the constrictions of cultural conditioning." Jessie's feelings about marriage within a sexist society as an institution that "locked women in growth-retarding roles" also informed her stories. No doubt this knowledge influenced her own actions and may have contributed to her decision to marry so late in life and to maintain an active career thereafter. And so she struggled, wanting to get her message out, realizing that it would never be read and that she herself would be rejected unless she couched her message in the most conventional of terms or, conversely, presented her characters as exotic, primitive, uninhibited creatures to white audiences eager for titillation. It was still white men who held the publishing purse strings.

But brave Jessie hadn't changed much from that first day at Philadelphia High School for Girls. She dared to write, albeit timorously, about black women who claimed responsibility for their own lives and did what they wanted rather than what was expected of them. It still remains for future readers to truly appreciate Jessie's body of work.

There can be no doubt about her contribution to the development of African-American writers, especially women writers such as Alice Walker and Toni Morrison. Langston Hughes expressed his obligation thus: "Jessie Fauset at *The Crisis*, Charles Johnson at *Opportunity*, and Alain Locke in Washington were the three people who midwifed the so-called New Negro literature into being. Kind and critical—but not too critical for the young— they nursed us along until our books were born."

Her legacy continues to inspire today.

ALICE STOKES PAUL
1885–1977

Mother of the Equal Rights Amendment

You, over whom the jeers and the mocking and the ugly
thoughts
Of those who understand not
Pass lightly, like a spent breath of foul air in a still cavern,
Unflicking the steadfast torch of you—
I could re-light forever the waning fires of my courage
At the incessant, upleaping flame of your being!

> —Elizabeth Kalb
> *The Suffragist*, January 25, 1919

*A*lice sat alone in her cell in the psychiatric ward. Her
arms were as thin as a child's, her eyes huge in her pale, emaciated
face. After vomiting continually while being force-fed, she had
fainted and been dragged back to her cell. Her throat ached and her
head pounded with a pain worse than migraine. This separation
from her compatriots was a new form of torture. When the prison
psychiatrist had been called in to see her, she had roused herself

Alice Stokes Paul

enough to speak for an hour on the history of suffrage. Impressed, the doctor said, "There is a spirit like Joan of Arc. . . . She will die, but she will never give up." Still looking for a way to break her spirit, the prison guards had ignored this admiring report and had moved Alice to the insane ward. They had boarded up one of her windows and had replaced her wooden door with a grated one. All day long mentally ill patients stared in at her; all night they screamed. And even when Alice covered her ears, those screams echoed in her head. Every hour throughout the night a nurse flashed a bright light in her face. She was barely able to keep her sanity with only a couple of hours of sleep a night, if that. Slumping against the wall next to her bed, Alice watched the cockroaches scuttle back and forth across her cell floor, helping themselves to her foul cup of drinking water. She was so cold, and the damp made her bones ache. She pulled the filthy unwashed blanket over her legs in a vain attempt to keep warm. The food they had brought her sat untouched in the corner; worms crawled on top of the rice and watery soup. The superintendent had ignored the doctor's orders for milk, toast, and medicine. She had been allowed no visitors, no mail, no reading matter. She longed to speak to an attorney, but the prison superintendent had not allowed any of the protesters to be visited by counsel. Alice closed her eyes. No tears, no tears. Her throat hurt so much where they had pushed the feeding tube down into her stomach. She wished she could hear the whispers and laughter of her comrades. She needed their support, their love. Was she dying? Well, then, she would die for victory. Alice's eyes drifted shut, and for a little while she slept.

Alice Stokes Paul was born on a 214-acre farm in Burlington County near Moorestown on January 11, 1885, the oldest child of William Mickle and Tacie Parry Paul. Her father was a prosperous farmer and banker. Her mother came from a long line of Quaker activists. Alice's maternal grandfather was president of Rutgers

University and a co-founder with Lucretia Mott of Swarthmore College, where Alice's mother was one of the first students.

Alice's Quaker beliefs informed her entire upbringing. She was taught to live simply, to refer to others as *thee* and *thou*, and to spend many hours in silent search for her own deepest conscience and inner truth. At the same time, she was exposed to the rightness of protest and civil disobedience as a child when her mother took her to suffrage meetings at a neighbor's house.

Alice's education was prodigious for a woman at the turn of the nineteenth century. At the age of sixteen she entered Swarthmore College on a scholarship, where she pursued sports and studied biology, economics, and political science. She graduated Phi Beta Kappa in 1905. After training as a social worker on New York's Lower East Side, she graduated from what is today the Columbia University School of Social Work. She then earned a master's degree in economics and sociology at the University of Pennsylvania. This was followed by studies in England at the Woodbrooke Settlement for Religious and Social Study, the University of Birmingham, and the London School of Economics. Alice also received a Ph.D. from the University of Pennsylvania. In 1922 she received a bachelor of laws degree from the Washington College of Law, a master of laws degree from American University in 1927, and a doctor of civil law degree from American University in 1928.

It was during her time in England that Alice found her life's work. Women's suffrage had been an issue there since the 1860s, but little progress had been made. Dissatisfaction grew when such tired methods as parlor meetings and petitions failed to move suffrage along. In 1903 a new organization was formed by Mrs. Emmeline Pankhurst called the Women's Social and Political Union (WSPU). When two of its members heckled a leader of the Liberal Party, bystanders and police joined forces to attack the women, who were arrested. The uproar that followed this incident convinced the WSPU that it had discovered a new tactic. The members began to provoke violence on the part of police in order to embarrass party leaders into doing something about women's suffrage. In prison, prolonged and widely publicized hunger strikes leading to brutal force-feeding fanned the flames of militancy. Alice joined British suffragists as they marched through the streets and went on hunger strikes. During one of her prison terms Alice met lifelong friend Lucy Burns, a fiery redheaded Irish Catholic graduate of Vassar.

Ill from the effects of prison and strikes, pale and emaciated, Alice returned to the United States in 1910 to complete her doctoral dissertation on the legal status of women in Pennsylvania, but her struggles in England remained very much in the forefront of her thoughts. In 1912 she renewed her friendship with Lucy, who was just back from London, and the two dedicated themselves to re-creating the American suffrage movement along the English model.

In the United States the years from 1896 to 1910 were known among suffragists as "the doldrums." No new women's suffrage states were won, and only six state referenda were held. All were lost. There was no functioning national center and little visible activity. As Harriet Stanton Blatch, Elizabeth Cady Stanton's daughter, put it: "There did not seem to be a grain of political knowledge in the movement . . . but a great change was called for in the method of attack by the reformers themselves." Internal rifts drove wedges into the National American Woman Suffrage Association (NAWSA). Suffering from the lack of a clear-cut policy while suffragists clamored for action, each national convention saw major changes among officers and leadership. Victories in Washington state and California had aroused new and virulent opposition to women's suffrage. Women had won full suffrage in nine states with a total of forty-five electoral votes, but none of these states was of essential political importance. The question the National Association was asking itself was whether a state-by-state attack was the right course to continue to pursue. Women's suffrage had not been debated on the floor of the Senate since 1887 and had never reached the floor of the House of Representatives. The time was ripe for a charismatic leader with new ideas to step in— and Alice was ready.

Alice and Lucy persuaded Jane Addams to intervene on their behalf with the NAWSA leadership to put them in charge of the organization's congressional committee. Once in place, they recruited other like-minded women to form the Congressional Union (CU), devoted exclusively to the fight for a federal amendment. Alice and Lucy came to Washington, D.C., in January 1913. There they rented a basement room on F Street Northwest, the first office of the CU.

Within two months the tiny group had organized a parade of 8,000 women. Though Alice herself was not a dramatic person, she could create drama in order to reach her goals. The women wore costumes and carried banners. Leading the parade in flowing white robes astride a white horse was lawyer Inez Milholland Boissevain, followed by floats and marching units. Alice had chosen the day before Woodrow Wilson's inauguration, a day she knew would be filled with visitors from all over the country, to stage the parade. When the president-elect reached Washington and saw no welcoming crowds, he was said to have asked where the people were. They were over on Pennsylvania Avenue, he was told, watching the suffrage parade, where the "Great Demand" banner was carried for the first time. It read: WE DEMAND AN AMENDMENT TO THE CONSTITUTION OF THE UNITED STATES ENFRANCHISING THE WOMEN OF THE COUNTRY. It would be carried at every parade, protest, and march until the Suffrage Amendment was passed. Although the marchers had a police permit, the surging crowd completely overwhelmed

Washington police and overran the marchers. A near-riot ensued, with the women being taunted and insulted and barely able to complete their march. Public opinion was outraged, and priceless publicity was garnered by this first of many protests. The CU had picked up momentum.

Though Suffrage Association leaders welcomed the new upsurge of interest in the federal suffrage amendment, a feeling of uneasiness grew, especially among more conservative members. Eventually a rift developed between the NAWSA and the CU, sparked by severe disagreements concerning methods and aims. At the 1913 suffrage convention, the CU demanded an all-out campaign for passage of the federal suffrage amendment. The much more conservative NAWSA leadership felt that such a campaign was extremely premature. Alice and the CU continued to insist that all suffrage work be limited to pressure on Congress and the president for a federal amendment. The CU also refused to submit to limitations on their activities by NAWSA policy. Compromises between the two factions failed as the deep differences in policy continued to grow. Finally Alice was removed as chair of the CU. Lucy and others resigned, and in February 1914 the two organizations split. Attempts were later made to heal the split, but the CU's insistence on holding the "party in power"—in this case the Democrats—responsible for failure to pass the suffrage bill conflicted with more moderate suffragists' belief that no one party could be held responsible and that doing so would alienate those in the majority party who supported women's suffrage. Alice answered that since President Wilson was a Democrat and the Democrats had a majority in both houses of Congress, they could have put suffrage through if they wanted to. "We have to make them want to," she declared.

As the NAWSA continued its plodding, state-by-state agenda, the CU moved into higher gear across the country. During the 1914 election campaign, it sent organizers into nine western states that had won equal suffrage in order to swing the women's vote against Democratic candidates whether or not they were suffrage advocates. The message was clear: Women voters had power—and they would use it!

In spring 1915 Alice and the CU began organizing in every state. Half a million signatures were gathered on another suffrage petition. At a rally in Washington and a march to the Capitol, the signatures were presented to President Wilson. Under Alice's stoic, hardworking leadership, the suffrage activists trudged ahead, giving life to an issue that, just shortly before, had been thought crushed. Even Carrie Chapman Catt, conservative leader of the NAWSA and no lover of Alice, gave her and the CU credit for raising the issue of suffrage from the dead.

There were others who didn't like Alice. Even her dear friend and comrade Lucy admitted that Alice's occasional abruptness lost some workers but felt that they were "the less fine spirits anyway." Alice could sometimes seem cold, remote, and austere because, according to Inez Haynes Irwin, "the fire of her spirit burns at such a heat that it is still and white. She has the quiet of a spinning top." Colleagues described her "burning sincerity" and called her "a Napoleon without self-indulgence." Fellow suffragist Maud Younger described Alice's devotion to the cause as self-sacrificing, her will as indomitable, her mind as clear, penetrating, and analytic, and her style as open, without suspicion. The small courtesies so important to some were not important to Alice, and she often forgot to thank people when they said yes. It must not have occurred to her that others might need these small acts of courtesy. After all, she was not asking for herself, she was asking for Suffrage.

Some said that Alice was blind to the situation of black women in the United States. That is doubtless untrue about a person as well educated and informed as Alice, who was also steeped in Quaker beliefs of equality. However, she would have done almost anything to achieve equal suffrage—and that included maintaining the support of white Southern women for the amendment. To hold that support, Alice made decisions that, in hindsight, seem racist. Before the suffrage parade outside the White House in 1913, Alice expressed sympathy for black women's suffrage. Yet when the parade began, suffrage leaders asked Ida B. Wells not to march with the Chicago delegation, concerned that her presence would offend Southern white women. Black women were often denied the right to speak at National Women's Party (NWP) meetings, the excuse being that there was not room on the schedule for them.

In 1921 Alice responded to mounting pressure, and the NWP permitted a representative of African-American women a place at the unveiling of the statues of suffragists in the Capitol Rotunda. Alice also willingly agreed to have the issue of the disenfranchisement of black women raised at the convention that was to follow. When queried on race issues, pragmatic Alice answered that the NWP policy was always to concentrate on its own issue and not take up others. It was a fact that the NWP was continually besieged by more than fifty different groups desiring it to take up various causes and that addressing all of them might have weakened the successful drive for equal suffrage.

Alice didn't ask anything of anyone that she wouldn't ask of herself. The policeman on the beat said that a light burned in suffrage headquarters all night long. There were times that Alice worked all day, all night, and into the next morning. She lived in a cold room so that she would not be tempted to stay up late reading her favorite detective novels. When she picketed, she often took a stenographer with her so that she could dictate while on picket duty. According to comrades, she wasted no time on side issues, petty hostilities, or rivalries. Her knowledge of political processes was prodigious and prescient, and she worked toward her goal with a single-mindedness that was awe inspiring, regardless of the consequences or the sacrifices. Personally shy, Alice never married or had children. Indeed, first women's suffrage and later the Equal Rights Amendment were her children.

In summer 1916, facing a presidential election and with the entire House of Representatives and one-third of the Senate at stake, the CU, now renamed the National Woman's Party (NWP), organized in the twelve states where women had the vote. It was strongly felt that women's votes might determine the presidency of the United States. In any case, that is what Alice and her colleagues wanted Congress and the president to believe. The thought struck fear and respect into the hearts of politicians previously deaf to suffragists' entreaties. And although no specific comments were made on the Suffrage Amendment, individual candidates did refer to the desirability of women's suffrage in their campaigns.

Alice and the NWP kept up a relentless pressure on President Wilson and maintained a strong anti-Democratic position. But when this tactic failed to produce the desired results (Wilson carried ten out of twelve "suffrage states"), there seemed no choice but to turn to militancy. While the NAWSA continued its state-by-state drive and the NWP continued to lobby the president and Congress, on January 10, 1917, the first suffrage pickets, called Silent Sentinels, stood outside the gates of the White House holding banners that read MR. PRESIDENT, WHAT WILL YOU DO FOR WOMEN'S SUFFRAGE? and HOW LONG MUST WOMEN WAIT FOR LIBERTY?

The women stood outside the White House day after day as relations with Germany deteriorated. It seemed possible that the United States would become involved in a terrible global war that had already decimated Europe. Suffragists looked on anxiously, aware that entrance into a war would have terrible repercussions on the suffrage battle. Here again, the NAWSA and the NWP split bitterly over tactics, with the more conservative NAWSA ultimately devoting much time and energy to the war effort and the more radical NWP focusing solely on the suffrage drive. This was not surprising, given that much of the leadership of the NWP were Quakers. Still, as the United States became embroiled in the war, the NWP began using wartime events on its banner slogans, sharply reminding onlookers, the press, and Congress that slogans advocating democracy were empty when there was none at home. The women even went so far as to refer to the president as "Kaiser Wilson." Antisuffragists kept up a steady stream of propaganda, trying to make the public believe that the suffragists were traitors to their country when they would not stop their suffrage work in time of war. Mobs of hoodlums, some in uniform, began attacking the pickets until, on June 22, 1917, the arrests began.

Throughout the more than six months of arrests, the only charge ever made was that the women obstructed sidewalk traffic. The pickets never violated any law or committed any crimes. Their arrests were, in fact, illegal but were countenanced under a severe curtailing of civil rights and liberties during wartime. The men (including police) who tore their banners, spit on the women, and threw them to the ground were never arrested.

In the beginning Alice and her comrades were dismissed without sentencing. But as picketing and violence continued, the courts began sentencing the women to jail time, with terms increasing from a few days to six months. Alice herself was tried and sentenced to seven months in prison. She was placed in solitary confinement with nothing to eat but bread and water. Weakened and unable to walk, she was ultimately taken to the prison hospital, where she began her hunger strike and was forcibly fed. In all, 218 women from twenty-six states were arrested, and 97 went to prison. Many were professionals; some were old, some barely sixteen. Some were wealthy wives of prominent men; many were college graduates, and a large number were working women. They served their time in the horrible Occoquan workhouse in Virginia or in the District of Columbia jail. November 15, 1917, called the Night of Terror by the imprisoned suffragists, was the most frightening for the women. Under orders from Superintendent W. H. Whittaker, forty guards with clubs went on a rampage, beating thirty-three suffragists, chaining their hands to the cell bars, smashing their heads against the iron beds, and dragging, choking, and kicking them. Brutalized and angry, the women protested against their illegal arrests and the life-threatening conditions of their incarceration by refusing to eat the worm- and cockroach-infested food. The prison authorities then resorted to forced feeding. Ultimately this treatment made martyrs of the women and helped tremendously to move the suffrage cause along.

Alice and the other women were done a great injustice, one for which this country never adequately apologized. Alice and her sisters-in-arms were illegally denied counsel, visits from family or friends, reading matter, decent food, clean bedding, and medical care. Still, they persevered. There seemed an endless supply of women ready to take the place of an arrested picket. As time went on, Wilson could no longer continue to claim ignorance of the women's imprisonment and mistreatment. Alice demanded that she and the others be given the status of "political prisoners." The Wilson administration refused, claiming that it would create "hazardous wartime precedents." But by now, with the prisoners continuing their hunger strikes, the nationwide outcry against the treatment of wives, daughters, and mothers had reached a crescendo. On November 27 and 28, all pickets were unconditionally released, and in March of the following year, every prison sentence and arrest was invalidated.

In January 1918 the House of Representatives passed the Suffrage Amendment 274 votes to 136, exactly the two-thirds majority needed to pass a Constitutional amendment. Fifty-six of the men who had voted against the amendment in 1915 changed their votes to "aye." The majority of the "nay" votes came from the South and from the industrial states of Massachusetts, Pennsylvania, Ohio, and Alice's own home state of New Jersey. Eighteen months later, the Senate passed the Suffrage Amendment in June 1919.

It was now necessary to secure ratification by the legislatures of thirty-six states. Many believed this would take *another* seventy years. Alice thought differently and continued to campaign until the thirty-sixth state ratified in August 1920. On August 26 Alice stood proudly over a long gold, white, and purple silk banner that had been unfurled from the second-floor balcony of the NWP headquarters in Washington, D.C. Alice herself had sewn on the last star (for Tennessee) of thirty-six stars representing each of the thirty-six states that ratified the Suffrage Amendment.

Even though women had the vote, Alice could not rest. By the 1920s it was clear that the drive toward reform had slowed significantly. The Supreme Court struck down minimum-wage laws in 1923. The campaign to win women the right to serve on juries ended in the face of opposition. Women were not voting even though they now had the right, and huge political forces were rending the women's movement asunder. A major emphasis on patriotism engendered by the war and the Bolshevik Revolution in Russia tore apart the progressive coalition of the prewar years. Even the Parent Teachers Association and the General Federation of Women's Clubs were accused of trying to establish communism in America. General Amos Fries, head of the Chemical Warfare Service, produced a chart in the form of a spider's web, describing the interconnectedness of American women's organizations and alleging that these groups intended to foment a Communist revolution in the United States. The list included every major women's organization and twenty-nine of the most prominent women leaders.

The backlash from the "spider's web" propaganda weakened the women's movement. Growing divisions within finished it off.

In 1921 the NWP called a convention to talk about where the women's movement should go after attaining the vote. Every major women's organization sent delegates except the NAWSA. Various leaders pressed such concerns as protective labor legislation, birth control, black women's right to vote in the South, and the peace movement. Alice rejected all, arguing that the focus should be on a "purely feminist program" concerned only with removing all laws that continued to deny women freedom. Alice was concerned solely with how women's lives were constricted by law. In many states women were denied equal pay for equal work, denied the right to serve on juries, and the right to work as public officials or to be employed at certain jobs. Wives could not have their own income without their husband's permission; they could not make contracts, choose where they lived, or have equal guardianship over their children. Alice felt that changing each law piece by piece would require endless and possibly futile effort. Instead, she reasoned, why not go after these restrictive laws the same way women had gone after equal suffrage—through a Constitutional amendment that would secure, by law, women's equality with men. In 1923 the NWP introduced an Equal Rights Amendment (ERA) into Congress, written by Alice, which read: "Men and women shall have equal rights throughout the United States and every place subject to its jurisdiction."

This seemingly simple statement caused a revolution in the ranks of feminists. Practically every women's organization in the country opposed the amendment. Reformers claimed that the ERA would get rid of protective labor laws that helped more women than they hurt. Alice and her supporters saw women and men as being alike, sharing the same needs and aspirations. They asked women to subordinate issues of class, ethnicity, race, religion, and politics, distilling all these down to a "pure" sense of themselves as women. But trade unionist colleagues attacked the NWP as class-biased, a bunch of rich women unconcerned about the plight of poor women or women of color. Those opposed to a federal amendment saw men and women as decidedly different, with women as vulnerable and needing special protective laws. After all, women got pregnant and had children. Who would protect them? Even Alice's old comrade, Jane Addams, was opposed, arguing that Alice's fight for the ERA was a function of her "ignorance of society and life." Alice felt that protectionist laws hampered women's opportunities, continuing the culturally enforced perception that homemaking was women's primary desire, to the exclusion of work outside the home. Alice led the fight for equal rights by forming alliances with national women's organizations such as business and professional women's clubs and industrial workers. On the state level, Alice and a NWP committee of twelve attorneys identified discriminatory laws state by state and by 1929 had introduced nearly 600 bills to state legislatures. About half passed. Alice did not live to see a federal amendment guaranteeing equality for men and women pass, but she never stopped working, leading the fight for the ERA for forty-eight years.

Alice also devoted herself to an international fight for women's rights. She led the NWP to found the Inter-American Commission for Women in the Pan American Union. Throughout the 1930s at the League of Nations in Geneva, her association of women's groups from many countries achieved official League of Nation status. Alice also headed a Committee of Experts that produced hundreds of surveys of legal codes pertaining to women in each member nation. In 1938 Alice founded the World Women's Party (WWP). She and the party lobbied for equality in nationality laws, more women members in league delegations, and passage of the Equal Rights Treaty. The WWP headquarters in Geneva became a refugee center for feminists and liberal leaders stranded by wartime. When the situation became too dangerous, Alice returned to Washington.

Alice led the WWP in a successful struggle to include wording about sex equality in the United Nations Preamble, in several sections of the charter, and in the United Nations Universal Declaration of Human Rights. Another major victory for Alice came at the age of seventy-nine when, in 1964, pressed by her and the groups she led, Congress added the word *sex* to the equality clauses in Title VII of the Civil Rights Act. At the age of eighty-seven, Alice was still lobbying for ratification of the ERA. She died on July 9, 1977, at the age of ninety-two in the Quaker Greenleaf Nursing home in Moorestown, New Jersey. Her brave heart had finally failed.

Alice Paul was a warrior in the truest sense of the word. Determined to succeed at a task of immense proportions, she forfeited, as soldiers do, the pleasures and rewards of life we take for granted. There were no love affairs, no marriage, no children, and no personal wealth for her. She might have had personal regrets; if she did, she didn't dwell on them. It fell to her to be "useful," brave, and single-minded and to be in the forefront of the battle for equality and opportunity for women and generations of their daughters to come.

ALICE HUYLER RAMSEY

1886–1983

Pioneer Endurance Driver

*A*ll had gone fairly well until Iowa. But now torrential downpours had turned dirt roads into quagmires of heavy, bottomless muck. In order to keep the Maxwell car going, Alice had to keep the straining machine in low gear. The overheated engine, pushing too hard, boiled over constantly. They were out of water, and not a farm was in sight. Alice and her three cross-country traveling companions were exhausted and filthy, but the automobile had to be taken care of. Next to them on the road, the rainwater had gathered in muddy ditches, but without a pail or bucket, how would they get the water into the car?

Alice's sister-in-law, Nettie, soon proved the old axiom that necessity is the mother of invention. Nettie reminded her companions about the lovely cut-glass bottles with sterling silver tops that held their traveling toilet articles. They had seemed needlessly luxurious when the women left New York City, and they were awfully small. Nevertheless, said Nettie, it would only mean more trips to fill them up.

Without hesitation, they opened the beautiful leather cases and removed the silver lids and the contents of the jars. Gathering

Alice Huyler Ramsey

up their long, rain-soaked skirts, the women filled the bottles with muddy water—back and forth, back and forth, hour after hour as they looked for a village where they could rest the engine and add to their supplies of water and oil. Finally, soaking wet, filthy, bedraggled, exhausted, and unable to reach a town because of the heavy rains, the women raised the top of the auto, attached the curtains and the windshield, tucked themselves into the seats as best they could, and slept until morning. If "Operation Cut Glass" was to be as bad as it got, thought Alice, they would make it into the West, no matter what.

Alice Huyler was born on November 11, 1886, in Hackensack, New Jersey, the second child of John Edwin Huyler and Ada Mumford Farr. Alice's father, descended from Dutch settlers in Bergen County, was a lumber and coal dealer, steam launch captain, and later a fire chief. Her mother was a homemaker and an expert quilter. Alice attended Union Street Elementary School and Hackensack High School, from which she graduated in June 1903. Early on, Alice showed a remarkable aptitude for mechanics and a curiosity about the inner working of devices. Her father, considered a mechanical whiz, flew in the face of Victorian proprieties and encouraged Alice in her mechanical endeavors. Alice said of her father, "He had magic in his fingers, understood my interests and encouraged me." Unlike other girls of her time, Alice took the shop course in high school rather than the studies in "feminine art."

After graduation Alice attended Vassar College. Although Alice loved Vassar and found college life one of "endless happiness," she was already engaged to John Rathbone Ramsey (whom Alice affectionately called "Bone") when she began her college years. Not wanting to postpone marriage, nineteen-year-old Alice left college after two years to marry the established attorney and county clerk, who was in his mid-forties. Their first child, John Rathbone Ramsey Jr., was born in 1907.

By all accounts, Alice was an energetic and lively young bride, lucky enough to be married to an indulgent and forward-thinking husband. Alice described him as keeping an open mind and said he "never fenced me in." Indeed, though he never understood why she wanted to go off adventuring, the fact that she did want it made him want it for her. After a terrifying episode with her rig, during which Alice's horse was frightened by a Pierce-Arrow motor car, Bone decided that Alice would be safer driving an automobile. He surprised her with a fire engine–red Maxwell roadster upholstered in red tufted leather, which she learned to drive in only two lessons.

She was thrilled—commenting on the beauty of its interior, bucket seats, and handy rear jumpseat. Alice immediately discovered all she could about the mechanical aspects of the car, fascinated to learn how it operated and determined to maintain it in excellent running condition. Bone himself did not know how to drive, was nonmechanical, avoided travel, and felt great trepidation about being a passenger. He was heard to say about each new car they subsequently owned, "How do you stop this thing?"

Learning to drive was high on Alice's list of priorities, and a man from the local car agency was selected as her teacher. Lesson number one was conducted on the local streets of Hackensack. Lesson number two almost didn't take place because the teacher, Billy Wood, needed to drive to Pelham Manor in New York. However, he decided to ask Alice if she wanted to accompany him. Not surprisingly, she ended up driving the entire way. This was her second, and last, lesson, for Alice was then deemed experienced enough to go out on her own. That summer Alice drove 6,000 miles for fun, gaining experience on all types of roads and exploring the highways of New Jersey and surrounding areas.

Fascination with motoring had grown quickly in the United States. New Jersey was a center for many of the automobile sporting events that attracted interest in the early days. Races, endurance runs, and other competitions were held frequently and often sponsored by the New Jersey Automobile Association (NJAA). The first United States hill-climbing contest took place in West Orange in 1901. The NJAA also promoted dirt-track races in Newark in 1904—the winner covering 10 miles in just under sixteen minutes to win a huge silver trophy.

Alice organized and became president of the Women's Motoring Club of New York and won many first-in-class trophies. In 1908 she participated in an endurance run to Montauk Point, Long Island, New York, designed to demonstrate the reliability of various types of automobiles. After successfully reaching Montauk Point, Alice had the opportunity to speak with Cadwallader W. (Carl) Kelsey, sales manager for the Maxwell-Briscoe car company. Kelsey, openly admiring of Alice's skill with automobiles and ever mindful of the importance of publicity, proposed to Alice at a driving awards dinner that she become the first woman to drive an automobile across the United States "from Hell Gate on the Atlantic to the Golden Gate on the Pacific . . . and in a Maxwell!" The overland journey had been completed by only a handful of men, and Alice, if she took on the challenge, would be the first woman to accomplish the feat.

By 1909 the automobile industry had experienced enormous growth (124,000 cars had been sold by more than 290 manufacturers—but fewer than 6 in Hackensack). There was sufficient interest in autos on a practical level to have initiated the formation of the American Automobile Association (AAA) in 1902, founded to protect motorists, assist them with complicated legislation, design maps, and offer aid on the road. The New Jersey Automobile Club had been founded two years earlier. Still it was assumed that men were the only ones capable of driving. A doctor at the time had stated that "a speed of 15 or 20 miles an hour in a motor car causes [women] acute mental suffering, nervous excitement and circulatory disturbances . . . extending into the night and causing insomnia." This opinion was shared by many men, who registered their fears about the consequences of women's emergence from the home into the public realm. Similar to antisuffrage rhetoric, anti–women drivers propaganda claimed that women would neglect housekeeping, ignore their children, ruin their marriages, cause mixing of the classes and races, and degrade public morals if they ventured into automobiles (or the polls).

Early motoring was very dirty work. Men were allowed to dress for the act of driving—heavy overalls and sensible hats. But women were still expected to look "feminine," and that meant long skirts. It also meant a motoring coat—a hot and heavy creation made of leather, rubber, or fur—goggles, and heavy veils or a motoring mask made of mica with a translucent linen veil.

Early motoring also illuminated powerful differences in class. Women who had advantages of wealth and social status were the only ones who could challenge the male monopoly of the automobile. Most cars sold for more than $1,000, and who would have the gall to challenge Mrs. Morgan, Mrs. Whitney, or Mrs. Vanderbilt if they decided to take a spin in the family's new automobile? After all, their private chauffeur could drive them wherever they wanted to go. And while Alice was not in that league, she was comfortably upper middle class, with enough social standing in her community to thumb her nose at propriety and indulge her interest in mechanics and adventure.

Carl Kelsey wanted to refute the outrageous notions about women and driving—and he wanted to sell cars. If a woman could make a cross-country drive safely—and in one of his vehicles—his promotional campaign would be a smashing success, and future sales would be assured. And if it could be proved that women could drive as skillfully as men and without harm, sales would improve even more.

At first Alice was flabbergasted by Kelsey's praise of her skill and his proposed plan, but she thought "it sounded like a magnificent adventure." At the age of twenty-one, she had enormous energy and determination. And so, after talking it over with Bone (who was quite supportive for a man in any age, but especially in one with lingering Victorian attitudes) and arranging for John Jr. to be cared for by a nursemaid, Alice accepted the proposition and began to plan her daring cross-country adventure. She would be accompanied by Bone's two sisters, Margaret (Maggie) Atwood and Nettie Powell, both in their late forties, and by her friend Hermine

Jahns. Alice had described her two sisters-in-law as "well-groomed and dressed in the daintiest of French-heel footgear . . . conservative and reserved to the nth degree." Still, beneath the façade of Victorian propriety must have beaten the hearts of adventurers. Aside from Alice, none of these women knew how to drive or maintain a car. This would indeed be a challenge, for in 1909 there were few roads outside very large cities and only a handful of gas stations in the entire country.

Regardless of their audacity, Alice and her traveling companions would not be completely alone on their trip. The Maxwell-Briscoe Company arranged for their agents along the way to have tires, gasoline, and spare parts available for the travelers. They also hired John D. Murphy, automobile editor of the *Boston Herald*, as Alice's advance man. Paralleling Alice's trip, Murphy was to go on ahead of Alice and her companions by train and at prearranged stops take care of details, engage mechanics, and, hopefully, locate hotel rooms and food.

The starting point for this historic trip was the Maxwell showroom in Manhattan. Flashbulbs popped as Alice and her traveling companions posed in front of the forest-green open touring car in full driving regalia, including long, full skirts and rubber ponchos as well as rubber helmets with detachable goggles. They graciously accepted bouquets of carnations from the Elks Lodge of Hackensack. Reporters shouted questions at the women, particularly curious as to whether they planned to take a gun for protection. Alice answered that they had rejected the idea and added that she and her companions were "not afraid." In the pouring rain, Alice started the motor with a crank (a very dangerous contraption that had caused many fatalities), ran to the right-hand driver's seat to adjust the spark and throttle, waved to the crowd of family and friends huddled beneath umbrellas, kissed Bone goodbye, and was on her way, protective tire chains clanking noisily on the wet road.

On the first day Alice drove 70 miles to Poughkeepsie, New York. In addition to the four ladies, the heavily laden Maxwell carried spare engine parts, tire chains, heavy steel spring leaves, a jack, a hand pump, tire irons, spare inner tubes, patch kits and two spare tires, a gallon water jug, a canvas water bag, a camera, a small Sterno stove, and a hamper of food. Added later were a shovel, a towrope, and block and tackle. Each of the women was allowed one suitcase for "city" clothes and extra driving attire. One suitcase was little indeed in the days before synthetic and wrinkle-free clothing, and one long, full dress could just about fill a suitcase. Alice marveled that her traveling companions all managed to get huge flowered and beribboned hats into their suitcases, a feat more daunting to her than driving 3,800 miles. Alice wore only her one motoring cap with a stiff visor and a full crown.

The Maxwell itself was fitted with an oversized twenty-gallon gas tank installed beneath the front seat, a 30-horsepower engine that could reach speeds of 40 miles per hour, a calibrated wooden dipstick for the driver to check fuel levels, a glass tube on the dash through which to view the oil level, a speedometer, lanterns front and back that were lit by windproof matches, running boards on either side, chains for the rear wheels to bolster the treadless tires' traction in wet weather, a rubber bulb horn that honked when squeezed, side curtains and a folding leatherlike pantasote top, a hand brake, and a rear luggage rack. Alice would later say that although the Maxwell didn't have the speed or comfort of modern cars, "it was sturdy . . . I'm still proud of that Maxwell engine!"

Alice's mechanical and driving skill would stand her in good stead. Most roads were wagon trails—dusty in summer and muddy when wet, designed for horses, not engines. A collection of maps known as the Blue Book existed only for the eastern United States, but its usefulness was often limited, considering that there were few road signs and painted landmarks changed yearly.

Until the quartet reached the Mississippi River, crossing over an old wooden bridge and arriving at Fulton, Illinois, two weeks later, the trip was somewhat of a lark, despite a broken coil on the way to Buffalo, a blowout on the bumpy road to Cleveland, and a broken axle as they neared Chicago. Cities and towns the travelers had never seen whizzed by and, in Cleveland, the Maxwell actually reached 42 miles per hour, its highest speed of the trip. Their fame was already spreading; an eager crowd gathered at the Maxwell showroom in Chicago to wish them well.

Then the rain began. The constant downpours turned the road into a sticky quagmire. The narrow, smooth, slippery tires of the Maxwell doubled in size from the mud, and chains were of little help. The constant strain caused the engine to boil over repeatedly as the auto plowed ahead at a crawl over roads that Alice called "gumbo." Alice and her companions began to "wish we were on Noah's Ark." Finally it was decided that the Maxwell's load had to be lightened. Alice's three companions regretfully left the car with their baggage and heavy replacement parts and took the train to Sioux City, Iowa. John Murphy, Alice's advance man, took their place beside her as she gritted her teeth and pressed on. "I'll drive every inch of the way if it kills me," she said.

There was still more mud. It loosened bolts, damaged tires and axles, and shook the Maxwell to its core. Alice needed to be towed out of several mud holes. It took thirteen days to cross 360 miles of Iowa, and Nebraska wasn't much better. The women met up again, rested, refreshed, and with clean clothes, and the weather finally broke in Wyoming, bringing sunshine and huge ranches as far as the eye could see. To get through this land of privately owned, fenced pastures, crisscrossed with dirt trails, Alice's companions would jump from the car, open the gates that penned in the cattle or sheep, close the gate after the auto went through, and then jump back into the car.

At Ogallala, a grim set of uniformed men stopped the car. The women were alarmed. The man in charge asked if they had guns. Alice answered no and demanded to know what was going on. "Just a little murder," was the reply. The women waited two hours, wondering whether they were considered suspects. Finally they were told that the criminals had been apprehended, and once again they were on their way.

The scenery was beautiful, but the terrain was rough. Once the Maxwell had to descend into a 60-foot arroyo and climb up the other side. This required blocking the wheels every few inches over and over again until the long and tedious climb was completed. At Laramie permission was granted to cross a railroad trestle. Alice had to position the car on either side of the rail and navigate bumpy, dangerous miles high above a steep river chasm— and complete this maneuver before the train came through!

Across the Platte River, said Alice, the road "just plain quit." The group often became lost, and Alice followed telephone poles in the hope that the ones with the most lines would lead to a town. Sometimes they did. West of Salt Lake City, the intrepid group crossed endless miles of baking desert. Alice was eager to finish this part of the journey and on one day drove seventeen hours straight before taking a three-hour rest on a seat cushion thrown onto the desert floor. In Fish Springs, a tiny hamlet in the backcountry of Utah, the women finally had to stop for food after twenty hours of driving. The only meal available was one of dried cereal, tomatoes, and coffee. Making the best of a tough situation, Alice resolved "to accept what was at hand . . . and be thankful." Indeed, food was often a challenge on the long trip. The women often got along by eating a slice or two of bread with butter and sugar for nourishment and energy, but no one complained. They were, Alice said, "good sports . . . and accepted things as they came, lodging, food—even accidents!"

Along the way the women made a number of friends who helped them out. At Callao, Utah, a local blacksmith forged a new spring seat on their axle after it had hit a prairie dog hole. The blacksmith did a beautiful job, and the women were once again on their way.

The heat wave continued into Nevada—as did adventures. Ahead of them rode a dozen Indian braves, bare torsos gleaming in the hot sun. Their bows and arrows were drawn and seemingly poised for attack. (What a frightening sight this must have been for the urban-bred Eastern women!) The Indians suddenly wheeled their horses around and, with a series of fierce war whoops, charged in the direction of the four. Alice's heart "went down in the bottom of the car," but holding the steering wheel firmly, she attempted to "appear unafraid and keep right on going." As the band passed them by, they realized the Indians were only in hot pursuit of a jackrabbit. They were safe—and very much relieved.

Eventually the women reached the foothills of the Sierra Nevadas, the final serious obstacle. A steep climb over sandy roads zigzagged across the face of the mountains. The road was no highway but an old wagon trail. Traffic consisted of wagons and horses, mules, oxen, and men in the saddle. The Maxwell struggled to maintain speeds of less than 10 miles per hour. But what beauty: "We ran out of superlatives," said Alice, describing Lake Tahoe and the "exquisite loveliness of majestic sugar pines, Douglas firs and redwoods . . . blue skies and clear, sparkling water!" The beautiful Sierras behind them, the group entered California. At Oakland they boarded a ferry to San Francisco, where they were met by a cheering crowd and a cavalcade of cars. On August 7, 1909, fifty-nine days after she began the drive, Alice steered the Maxwell off the ferry toward a welcoming clamor of cheers and honking horns. She led a parade to a reception at the city's St. James Hotel before, lonely for her family, she returned to New York by train three days later.

Her reception at home must have been enthusiastic as well, for nine months later Alice gave birth to a daughter, named after her.

Despite Alice's feat and the resultant publicity for the reliability and comfort of Maxwell automobiles, the company was folded into the U.S. Motor Company in 1910, which went out of business two years later.

Alice's achievement, however, remains amazing. She personally patched or replaced at least a dozen blown tires by herself, cleaned sparkplugs with sandpaper and reassembled them, repaired the brake pedal and axles with pieces of wire, and endured sandstorms, broken springs, dirt, hunger, and fatigue to be the first woman to drive from ocean to ocean. She helped prove that travel by automobile was safe and reliable and opened up new pathways to see the country. "I see no reason why any woman who can drive a car cannot take one across the continent," she said.

Alice's interest in mechanics and driving never ceased. She was a prime organizer during World War I of the Red Cross Motor Corps for Camp Merrit in Dumont, which carried wounded from Fort Dix. She continued to take on mechanical projects, such as taking apart the crankcase of a Studebaker and reassembling it. In summer 1919 she resumed cross-country driving, taking her children on trips and ultimately driving cross-country more than thirty times after moving to California in 1948. In 1960 she was honored on the fiftieth anniversary of her cross-country drive by the Automobile Manufacturers Association as "First Lady of Automobile Travel" and was given the title "Woman Motorist of the Twentieth Century" by the American Automobile Association.

Ever undaunted, Alice took on the challenge of driving the six passes through the Alps in Switzerland at age ninety-four. A snowstorm closed the sixth pass, and her doctor forbade her to continue because of her pacemaker, no doubt a disappointment to this intrepid adventurer. Alice died on September 10, 1983, at age ninety-six. She had owned and driven more than twenty-five different automobiles, accident-free, with nary a mark on her driving record save for one ticket for making a U-turn. Always modest, the plucky Alice gave equal credit to others for her accomplishments. "I honestly think," she said, "the really brave ones were the husband who trusted in my ability, after only a year's experience at the wheel, and the three companions who put themselves in my hands to cross that long and little-known stretch of miles." Maybe. But without Alice, they never would have made it "from Hell Gate to the Golden Gate!"

MARIA JERITZA
1887–1982

Metropolitan Opera Star

*M*aria gazed wildly into the glowing footlights of the Metropolitan Opera's stage, her hair disheveled and her face stricken with anguish. At this moment she *was* Floria Tosca, lying prone at the feet of the wicked Scarpia, where she had fallen after their violent struggle.

The audience watched in disbelief as Maria did not arise. Instead the shimmering lines of "Vissi d'arte" filled the air. With heartbreaking emotion and beauty, Maria sang the entire Puccini aria from the floor, Tosca's torment deepening with every note as she agonized over a fate that had placed her and her beloved Cavaradossi into Scarpia's evil hands.

She finished to deafening applause, unlike any that the Met's general manager, Giulio Gatti-Casazza, had ever heard—the longest ovation he had witnessed in his entire career. Critic Deems Taylor echoed that "the theater broke out in a demonstration the equal of which I can scarcely recall." No one had ever portrayed Tosca like this before, and Maria had succeeded brilliantly on all levels—musical, theatrical, and emotional. It was a performance for the ages.

Maria Jeritza

Maria Jeritza was born on October 6, 1887, in Brunn, Austria, an area that later became part of Czechoslovakia. Born Mitzi Jedlicka, she changed her name sometime in her twenties during the rise of her operatic career.

Maria's passion for the drama that is an intrinsic part of the operatic tradition first became evident as a child. Although her sisters played house with "mere dolls," Maria's dolls were "characters" for whom she developed dramatic story lines.

Her parents came from modest financial circumstances, her father being employed as a concierge. Despite this lack of monetary resources, Maria's family managed to provide her early training in voice and drama at the Brunn Conservatory. She also served as an apprentice with the Brunn Opera, performing in the chorus.

Maria made her official operatic debut in 1910 in the Olmutz Opera Company, singing the role of Elsa in *Lohengrin.* The path to this event was an unusual one: Shy by nature, Maria always avoided auditions in formal settings—particularly those held in opera houses. Yet her teacher, Professor Auspitzer, believed that she had potential for an operatic career. Since Maria was reluctant to audition, the professor came up with a plan. He invited the manager of the Olmutz Opera to hide in another room and listen to Maria review repertoire from *Der Freischutz, Lohengrin,* and *Tannhauser.* When the visitor came out of hiding, Maria recalled that she "grew red in the face, stammered, did not know what to say." Professor Auspitzer laughed and commented: "Well, well, child . . . for once I have gotten the better of that incurable timidity of yours." Maria said that she "nearly fainted" when the Olmutz manager told her that she was hired. Maria was ultimately able to conquer her fears and was chosen to make her debut performing the role of Elsa. Her experiences with the company helped her gain perspective, and while she constantly worked to improve, she also had a touch of humor about things that went awry. "The first time I sang the 'Jewel Song,'" she recalled, "I lost so many notes that the cleaning woman must have found them scattered all over the floor the next morning when she started to scrub the stage."

Maria's association with the Olmutz Opera gave her enough confidence and experience to launch her career on broader horizons. She continued in the Wagnerian motif; after joining the Vienna Volksoper, she appeared as Elisabeth in *Tannhauser*. Her first appearance with this company was the result of an audition that consisted of performing just a few measures of Micaela's aria from *Carmen*. It took little for the auditioners to realize that hers was a major talent.

During Maria's time in Vienna she studied and coached with producer Max Reinhardt. He helped her interweave the notes of the score with the role's dramatic essence, giving equal emphasis to both. Maria studied the nuance of each character—from personality, to movements, to expressions, to costume—bringing even greater depth to her thoughtful musical approach. This combination of musicality and theatricality made her performances superb throughout her career.

Maria's two years with the Vienna Volksoper were important ones. She learned a vast amount of operatic repertoire and earned the respect and admiration of both audiences and opera administrators. The director of the company, Rainer Simons, thought so highly of her that he cast her in the world premiere of *Der Kuhreigen*.

Simons also attempted to cast Maria in Johann Strauss's *Ziguernerbaron*, to the marked protests of Strauss's widow and his publisher, Mr. Weinberger, both of whom believed that the role of Saffi should go to a more seasoned performer. Fortunately the opera's librettist, Ignaz Schnitzer, came to the rescue. He had heard Maria sing at rehearsals and was convinced of her musical capability for the role. She was permitted to perform, to everyone's delight—particularly that of Mrs. Strauss and Mr. Weinberger.

Emperor Franz Joseph was so captivated by Maria's perform-ance as Rosalinda in *Die Fledermaus* that she had to repeat the "Czardas" twice for him. "Where has Maria Jeritza been engaged that I have not heard her?" he demanded. His endorsement helped her gain an invitation to sing at the Vienna Hofsoper and the Vienna Imperial Opera.

In 1912 Maria was featured in another premier, *Aphrodite* by Max von Oberleithner. She made the role her own, not only vocally but also dramatically—in part by wearing a costume that gave the appearance of her being nude, causing a stir within the operagoing public. Throughout her career she demonstrated her willingness to take artistic and personal risks for the sake of authenticity, and her audiences loved it.

Subsequently Maria starred in numerous productions in opera houses throughout Europe—from Berlin, to Stockholm, to Odessa, and beyond—and her fabulous successes drew attention from several composers, leading to professional associations with them. Several created roles specifically for her and coached her within these roles to help maximize the full impact of each char-acter onstage. Maria was not afraid to speak her mind and to pro-vide composers with valuable feedback. Such an exchange occurred with Richard Strauss, who wrote *Ariadne auf Naxos* for her. Suppos-edly upon receiving the score, Maria told Strauss that the opera "would not do." He willingly revised it. It was also reported that during a rehearsal for the production, Maria departed from singing the score as written. When a bystander nervously asked whether Strauss might stop her, he replied, "Stop her? No, leave her alone, she knows what she's doing." Maria starred in the 1912 premier of the work with the Stuttgart Royal Opera.

Strauss later wrote other roles for her, including the leads in *Frau Ohne Schatten* and *The Egyptian Helene.* She received coaching from Strauss for numerous roles—notably Octavian in *Der Rosenkavalier.*

"I had to portray a young man in that opera," said Maria. "Herr Strauss spent hours teaching me the correct walk." These sessions gave her invaluable help in portraying such varied characters with realism and depth, and Maria was grateful to Strauss for his generous work with her.

Maria toured Europe with great success and continued to perform there throughout World War I, despite an invitation to appear at New York's Metropolitan Opera. This contract needed to be put on hold until the conclusion of the war, but the wait was well worth it for audiences in New York—although it was not until 1921, the season after the death of famed tenor Enrico Caruso, that Maria finally made her debut at the Met. She later revealed that "One of the great disappointments of my career in America has been the cruel fate, which robbed me of a chance to sing at the Metropolitan with Enrico Caruso."

For Maria the Met organization was a truly supportive team. Still, her shyness raised its head once more the night she debuted in front of an audience on that famous stage. Maria said that she had "never felt the same terror . . ."

On November 19, 1921, Maria sang the lead role of Marietta in the New York premier of *Die Tote Stadt* by Erich Wolfgang Korngold, a role she had previously performed in Europe. Since this was a relatively unfamiliar work, it was an unusual vehicle with which to begin a career at a new house in a new country. But her performance was remarkable. The *Musical Courier* carried a review with the headline: "*Die Tote Stadt* a success; Jeritza a Sensation." This also marked the first time since the war that an opera was sung in German at the Met. However, according to *Musical America*, this fact paled in comparison with the public's eagerness to see and hear Maria onstage. She became the toast of both New York and Vienna.

Maria consistently worked to improve her vocal and dramatic presentation, studying voice with the legendary Marcella

Sembrich and others. She held Sembrich in the highest regard, saying that she was "unquestionably a great teacher," although strict. "In all that concerns the grand tradition of the concert stage, she is a past mistress."

Maria worked at gymnastics and swimming to keep fit and thus was able to roll down the stairs in Mascagni's *Cavalleria Rusticana* without injury and engage in a credibly vigorous dance routine during Bizet's *Carmen*—and continued to perform such feats well into her sixties. Maria loved such dramatic touches, and they were a part of her trademark. Audiences especially loved the Act III scene in *Girl of the Golden West*, during which Maria actually rode a horse bareback onto the stage.

Opera's "golden age" was in full swing between 1910 and 1930. Singers were stars and received much attention and enthusiastic support from their fans—somewhat like the adulation given to modern-day movie and pop stars. The public faithfully attended performances featuring their favorite singers and eagerly read newspaper and magazine accounts about every feud, scandal, love affair, or misstep.

Maria provided plenty of fodder for fan magazines and rumor mills. Some say that Maria's arrival at the Met kindled a feud between her and longtime prima donna Geraldine Farrar that ultimately caused Farrar to leave. True or not, such rumors kept patrons eager for more. Henry T. Finck, newspaper critic of the *Evening Post*, commented on Maria's musicianship as well as her rivalry with Farrar. He felt that Maria had no wish to engage in a feud with Geraldine Farrar, venturing that perhaps this rumor had only been spread by a public eager for a good story about their favorite singers.

In addition to the reported feud with Farrar, incidents with other singers served to keep opera fans well supplied with behind-the-scenes drama. For example, one evening famed tenor Beniamino

Gigli evidently kicked Maria in the shins over curtain call priority. Maria appeared weeping at the stage footlights saying, "Mr. Gigli is not nice to me." Both reporters and fans loved every morsel of these stories, and this particular event received nationwide attention.

Gossip and feuds notwithstanding, there was no debate as to Maria's success at the Met. Her first appearance as Tosca on December 1, 1921, assured her fame. It was at this performance that she first performed "Vissi d'arte" while lying on the floor—an effect that received Puccini's seal of approval and brought the house down. The staging had literally come about by accident. Maria slipped during a dress rehearsal and chose to sing the aria from that position. Puccini himself ran to her afterward and said, "Carissima, you must always do it this way." Her inspiration, he told her, was "from God."

Although many other sopranos tried to copy this staging, none could equal Maria. She performed the aria the same way throughout her career, including her last performance of *Tosca* at Symphony Hall in Newark more than forty years later.

Floria Tosca became a signature role for Maria and was referred to by Olin Downes, critic for the *New York Times,* as a "sweeping triumph." Her drama, beauty, and glorious voice all blended together and catapulted Maria—already an acclaimed prima donna—to lasting fame.

Maria also toured the United States as a concert artist. Her repertoire ventured into a wide array of selections beyond traditional operatic fare and included such art songs as Debussy's "Beau Soir," Amy Beach's "Ah, Love, but a Day," and Frank La Forge's "Mexican Folk Song." She appeared in Baltimore, Washington D.C., Pittsburgh, Buffalo, Milwaukee, Cleveland, Chicago, and many other cities. Away from the stage she was a talented cook and loved the "picture shows."

During the Depression, opera houses did everything possible

to boost finances by expanding their repertoire to attract larger audiences. The Met was no exception. Much of this new repertoire and a number of the productions themselves did not catch on with the public. Maria was the rare exception, appearing in Franz von Suppe's *Boccaccio*, in which she sang "with verve," helping make such new additions to the company's repertoire appealing. Still, this was a tough time for the artistic world, as it was for everyone, and Maria's commanding salary, coupled with hard times, forced the Met to decide against renewing her contract.

Maria's years at the Met lasted until 1932. She had performed twenty different roles there over the years, including Tosca, Turandot, Carmen, Santuzza, and Manon. She frequently returned to Vienna and to other cities in Europe to sing and was a favorite on both continents during her Met years. A tall, beautiful woman with a crown of lovely blond hair, Maria was the quintessential prima donna in appearance as well as in bearing—a far cry from the shy girl who shunned live auditions in Europe. Her stage presence and sense of drama were legendary. She always threw herself heart and soul into anything she did, on the stage or off—and her audiences loved it.

Maria's life took a decidedly different turn after leaving the Met and upon her marriage to Winfield Sheehan in the mid 1930s. (A previous marriage to a European baron had ended in an annulment. However, Maria spoke warmly of her former mother-in-law, singer Blanche Marchesi.) Sheehan, a production executive for Fox Pictures in the growing motion picture industry, brought Maria to Hollywood. It was during this time that she became a U.S. citizen. The Sheehans lived on a ranch in Hidden Valley in California, where they entertained friends such as Will Rogers. Maria's attempt to star in films was brief and unsuccessful, but her live musical performances were still in demand. She sang at the Hollywood Bowl, in local concerts, and on the radio and remained active within musical circles. She loved her ranch as well as the Lippizzan horses she and Winfield owned. This idyllic period ended for Maria when Winfield Sheehan died in 1945.

Maria relocated to the East Coast once more and in 1948 married Irving (Pat) Seery, a Newark, New Jersey, businessman and manufacturer of umbrella frames. Seery, a long-standing opera fan, had been in the audience at Maria's Metropolitan Opera debut and was totally captivated from the beginning, attending her performances for many years. It was reported in one of her obituaries that Seery had purposely remained a bachelor for more than thirty years until she was free to marry him.

The Seerys moved to the beautiful Ballantine mansion in Newark, which they remodeled with exquisite taste. The mansion, located in the city's Forest Hill section at Elwood and Clifton Avenues, was a true palace—with a guest house, two carriage houses, and gardens in addition to the main house. Maria and Pat's parties were legendary and included a guest list that ranged from violinist Fritz Kreisler to former United Nations Secretary General Kurt Waldheim. According to one local observer, Maria was the life of any party she attended or hosted. On a smaller scale, Maria welcomed the local children to her home on both Halloween and Christmas Eve and distributed Viennese chocolate. The children never forgot her.

Despite the many beautiful residences that Maria maintained around the world, she always considered Newark to be her home and continued to live there for the rest of her life. From this location she contributed toward the rebuilding of the Vienna Staatsoper and St. Stephen's Cathedral after they were destroyed during World War II, and she traveled to Vienna every year between 1948 and 1954 to sing in benefit operas for these building projects.

Maria also worked on behalf of the Metropolitan Opera to benefit the Opera Guild, as well as for the New Jersey State Opera and other groups. She appeared as a guest with the New Jersey Symphony and other local groups. Maria sang her last *Tosca* at Symphony Hall in Newark during the mid 1960s to a sold-out house.

Pat Seery passed away in 1966, and Maria remained in Newark with her secretary, Liesel Hilfreich, as her companion.

Throughout her life Maria received numerous awards and honors for her contributions to the musical world—including those from monarchs, musical organizations worldwide, and the Vatican. These awards included the Legion of Honor and the Golden Grand Cross of Austria. She appeared before royalty and presidents and performed in most of the prestigious music houses worldwide. She was made an honorary member of the State Opera of Austria (formerly the Court Opera) and was recognized for her efforts on behalf of Austria by being made an honorary member of the Austrian section of the League of Nations.

Maria performed more than 200 operatic roles during her lifetime in five different languages. She was beloved by composers and audiences worldwide. The last song Strauss ever wrote was a gift to Maria, which he sent to her in 1949. The inscription read: "To my beloved Maria, this last rose!"

Maria did much for the arts within New Jersey. She received the first Governor's Award granted by the New Jersey Council on the Arts in 1971, given to her by then-Governor Brendan Byrne at a special reception at the governor's mansion. In 1978, as guest of honor at the New Jersey Opera Ball, she again met with the governor and danced with him. This was her last major public appearance.

Maria Jeritza died on July 10, 1982, at the age of ninety-four. Her gorgeous voice was stilled, but, in the words of Brendan Byrne, she would always remain "one of the world's great artists" as well as "one of New Jersey's most distinguished citizens."

HANNAH SILVERMAN

1896–1960

Hero of the 1913 Paterson Silk Strike

That's the Rebel Girl, that's the Rebel Girl!
To the working class she's a precious pearl.
She brings courage, pride and joy
To the fighting Rebel Boy.
We've had girls before, but we need some more
In the Industrial Workers of the World.
For it's great to fight for freedom
With a Rebel Girl.

—Joe Hill, 1915

Court Recorder James Carroll glared at the defiant girl. He hated these strikers. They would not back down, no matter how heavy a sentence he doled out for picketing. But this one, this teenaged Hannah Silverman, he would make an example of.

Hannah had been arrested *again* in Paterson, New Jersey, for following two female strikebreakers home from the silk mill. Frustrated by her resistance, Carroll wanted to break her spirit. Miss

THE NEW YORK PUBLIC LIBRARY

Hannah Silverman

Silverman, he ordered, would receive the incredibly stiff sentence of sixty days in the county jail. Hannah was unmoved. "Thank you, your honor," she replied, smiling at the judge. Taken aback, Carroll was uncertain how to respond. "You're welcome," he replied.

As Hannah and the five friends who had been arrested with her were marched to jail, they called out, "Three cheers for the IWW!" Hundreds lined their route, cheering the brave girls. And then they began to sing. They all knew the songs from the Industrial Workers of the World's *Little Red Songbook.* And everyone, including Hannah, knew how singing lifted the tired heart. "Come from every land / Join the fighting band / In one union grand" they sang.

Meanwhile, in Haledon Elizabeth Gurley Flynn of the IWW joked that "while this meeting is going on here another meeting is going on in Paterson and the police can't stop it either. That meeting is a gathering of our sisters and brothers at the county jail and they have good speakers such as . . . little Miss Silverman."

Seventeen-year-old Hannah was out on bail after only two days. Sure of her cause, Hannah threatened to take her case to the upper courts and to file suit for false arrest. The charge was quietly dropped and Hannah immediately went back to the picket lines. At a rally of more than 20,000 strikers the following Sunday morning, Hannah spoke stirringly to her fellow union members: "I've been to county jail three times already, but the police can't keep me away from the picket lines!"

Hannah Silverman, sometimes called Annie, was born on January 28, 1896, in New York City. Her mother, Sarah Sarna, was a Polish Jew, born in the textile manufacturing city of Lodz, Poland. Sarah was one of thirteen children of Hirsh and Fannie Sarna, who emigrated to the United States during the great influx of Eastern European Jews between 1881 and 1900. During that time it is estimated that about 600,000 Jews entered the United States to escape the Russian Pale of Settlement (Poland, Lithuania, Russia), where they were trapped by poverty and life-threatening anti-Semitic government decrees.

Jews were experienced veterans of class and labor struggle

and Jews from Lodz in particular had a reputation for being radical. Jewish textile workers carried their skills and revolutionary fervor from Lodz and other European manufacturing cities to the United States and to Paterson after the turn of the century. By 1910 there were between 3,000 and 5,000 Jews working in the silk industry.

Hannah's father, Morris Silverman, was an American-born Jew of German parentage. Sarah and Morris had four children, of whom Hannah was the second. When the Silvermans came to Paterson, an industrial city on the banks of the Passaic River, Morris may have hoped that because he was a German Jew their lives would be easier than those of the generally less well-educated Russian and Lithuanian Jews. But in Paterson there were actually two Jewish communities. The German Jews who had come from Germany in the late nineteenth century were often merchants or owners and managers of silk mills and part of a Jewish upper class. Newcomers from the Pale were looked down upon, and as they moved into Paterson's Jewish neighborhood, the German Jews moved to the fashionable East Side. The latecomers were generally given the lowest-paid work.

Little is known of Hannah's early years. But we can guess that her life was similar to that of other daughters of immigrant Jews. From a young age Jewish daughters, particularly those from the working class, were expected to take on serious responsibilities both at home and in the workplace. Housecleaning, cooking, and tending to younger children were all part of life. School was important, too, but daughters were expected to begin working at a very young age in order to help support the family. While this was difficult, it also gave them a social and personal freedom their mothers never had. Discovering that union work gave focus to her life, Hannah became part of a huge movement of Jewish working women who became famous for their rebelliousness and radical tendencies. Early-twentieth-century writer Hutchins Hapgood described women such as Hannah as "ghetto heroines . . . willing to lay down their lives for an idea, or to live for one."

Paterson, the seat of Passaic County located 15 miles west of New York City, was often referred to as the "Lyons of America." In the latter part of the nineteenth century and the opening decades of the twentieth, the city was a leading center in the manufacture of silk. With a ready supply of power from nearby waterfalls as well as proximity to ports and to New York's garment district, it was a natural location for this industry to grow and prosper. A steady flow of immigrants came to this gritty city looking for employment in the mills. By 1890 a third of Paterson's workers toiled in the silk industry, and by 1910 half its women were connected to the industry either as onsite employees or as piece workers. Frustration and anger at the working conditions in the mills, which paid the lowest wages of New Jersey's twenty-five leading industries, created continuous unrest and frustration. Workers knew they were not alone. From 1909 through 1916 labor conflicts continually erupted in the United States. Most important to the Paterson strikers, the 1912 Lawrence Massachusetts Textile Strike (called the "Bread and Roses" strike) of 20,000 workers had been won, serving as an example of what they, too, might accomplish.

A foreshadowing of future unrest in Paterson developed in 1912 with some brief but unsuccessful strikes. The situation came to a head on January 27, 1913, at the Henry Doherty Silk Company, where too much pressure to accept the four-loom system touched off fear and outrage that spread to other mills. Four employee committee members were fired at Doherty's mill that day after breakdowns in talks with management. As a result, 800 other workers walked out. By February 25 the entire textile industry in Paterson was on strike.

Solidarity in Paterson was reinforced by the presence and influence of the IWW, founded by Bill Haywood in 1905. The "Wobblies," as union members and leaders were called, encouraged revolutionary change from below rather than above. Perhaps most important, the IWW mobilized masses of working women, disregarding stereotypes of female delicacy and encouraging wives, mothers, and daughters to fight side by side with their men. And the IWW had Elizabeth Gurley Flynn, an experienced organizer who had first joined the IWW when she was sixteen and had quickly become a charismatic speaker. Only twenty-two in 1913, this "ordinary" girl was incredibly popular among young women, and unlike other IWW leaders she spent every day with the strikers, in the streets and in court. Encouraged by her example, many women who had been denied a role in public affairs seized the opportunity to take the stage. Of the 2,338 strikers arrested, one quarter were women, and they often refused bail in order to express their militancy.

Strikers were mostly immigrants from eastern and southern Europe and tended to form all-inclusive, industry-wide unions that bonded Jews and Italians, men and women. In Paterson they included the skilled broad-silk weavers (mostly non-English-speaking Italian and Jewish immigrants), the ribbon weavers (mostly English-speaking American citizens), and the unskilled dyers (mostly recent arrivals from Italy). The dyers were the humblest of the working classes, their working conditions the worst in the silk industry—and the most dangerous. As they added chemicals to silk yarn in large tubs, the steam and fumes were suffocating. Their feet, clad in clogs for protection, were always wet. Boiling chemicals burned the skin off their hands and ate off their fingernails. They often tasted mixtures to determine correct proportions, and early death from tuberculosis was frequent.

In Paterson the strike had been begun by the broad-silk weavers, who protested the doubling of loom assignments from two to four. This was known as a "stretch-out" and was a major threat to the workers. It entailed twice as much responsibility as their current jobs and foreshadowed layoffs and lower wages. However, it was the dyers who became the backbone of the strike. The basis for solidarity between skilled and unskilled workers centered on the movement for an eight-hour workday, an even wage scale with a minimum pay of $12 weekly, and representation by the IWW. The workers' platform also included an end to the oppressive "docking system" used against women apprentices, kickbacks in wages to foremen, and abuses in measuring the yardage of the finished product. Weavers in Paterson worked a ten-hour day and five hours on Saturday. Dyers worked eleven-hour days and thirteen-hour nights. And as the system sped up, wages were lowered. Paterson's workers were striking for a wage that had prevailed twenty years previously!

Although the strikers in Paterson would no doubt have held fast anyway, the actions of Paterson Police Chief John Bimson reinforced their early determination and cemented their unanimity. Throughout February and early March, Bimson sent patrolmen and mounted police to brutally break up assemblies and picketing and to prevent strike leaders from speaking at rallies at union halls, acting on the belief that the silk workers were puppets influenced by "outside" agitators. This was the final straw. How dare Bimson violate the workers' constitutional rights to freedom of assembly and freedom of speech! By the end of the second week, strike leaders estimated that 24,000 silk workers were out on strike, shutting down 300 silk mills. And the unity that followed Bimson's miscalculation lasted for almost five months.

Seventeen-year-old Hannah was employed at the Westerhoff mill on Van Houten Avenue when the strike began. She began picketing immediately and was first arrested on April 25. By that time she had become captain of the pickets at the mill and was called "the best known of the IWW pickets." She must have had a powerful presence for a young girl; on the occasion of her first arrest, the police asked Hannah to disperse the crowd before arresting her. After refusing to comply, she was charged with unlawful assembly and spent the night in the city jail. Instead of deterring her, this only cemented her determination and was the first of many arrests to follow.

Hannah seemed fearless. Two weeks after her first arrest, the "little agitator," as she was called by the assistant court prosecutor, was back in court for picketing the Westerhoff mill. When the prosecutor demanded that she tell the court what the IWW *really* was and if it was true that Bill Haywood *was* the IWW, Hannah shot back defiantly, "Haywood is Haywood. The workers in the mills are the IWW!" The *New York Times*, referring to Hannah as "pretty and intelligent," said "she proved a match" for the prosecutor in astuteness. Hannah further testified that she acted within the law and was not hostile to the authorities on the day of her arrest. When questioned whether or not an officer had asked her to disperse the crowd on April 25, she said yes, but added that she told him "it was his duty to do that!"

The following day Hannah watched from the rear of the court as Court Recorder James Carroll gave a brutally long sentence to a striker in another case. Some say she gasped; others say she hissed. Whichever was true, the furious Carroll slapped the girl he had previously called "impudent" with a twenty-day sentence for disorderly conduct. Her fellow strikers were concerned, as Hannah was supposed to lead a big parade to Madison Square Garden on the upcoming Saturday. But lawyers managed to arrange her release just in time for her to lead the procession. The *Paterson Evening News*, in its account of this and other legal proceedings concerning the strike, called Hannah "one of the leading lights in the present strike."

It was dangerous for Hannah and her fellow workers to be

strikers, even though, thanks to the strike leadership, there was little violence from picketers during the Paterson strike. (No strikebreaker was killed, no striker was found with a gun, and no policeman was maimed by a striker.) Hannah, who endured three terms in the Passaic County Jail (called the Paterson Bastile), tolerated two meals a day of sour bread, acidic coffee, and soup that often had dead insects in it. Her cell, where she spent thirteen and a half hours every day, was tiny, with poor ventilation and no sanitation. She shared a cup and a tub with nearly fifty other prisoners, some of whom had contagious diseases. Yet "the heroine of this strike," as she was called by Flynn, persisted willingly. This readiness to stand firm in the face of increasing intimidation angered both judges and prosecutors. As he gave her a suspended sentence, Judge Abram Klenert warned Hannah that if he saw her again he would put her in the State Home for Girls at Trenton until she was twenty-one.

Meanwhile, nonstrikers were urged by newspaper articles to join vigilante committees to stop picketing and drive out "agitators." Under a New Jersey blue law, anything said from a strike platform amounted to "inciting a riot" or "preaching anarchy"—both criminal offenses. An army of private detectives hired by mill owners, in particular the Weidmann Silk Dyeing Company, dogged the strikers and ultimately murdered two, one on a picket line and another as he sat with his child on the steps of his house. The killers were never brought to trial. Police attacked the strikers on horseback, clubbing them and calling them Wops or Jews. Then came arrests of the strikers, eventually numbering more than 2,200 arrests and 300 convictions. The police also jailed IWW speakers. Finally, city officials forbade mass rallies on Sunday within the Paterson city limits. Undaunted, the strikers moved their rallies to the neighboring town of Haledon, easily reached by trolley. The strikers used the second-floor porch of silk worker Pietro Botto's house to make their speeches to crowds of 30,000 or more people.

It was from the Botto house that speakers helped the workers to crystallize their understanding of the issues at hand, as well as to forge bonds of solidarity between the multiethnic, multiskilled groups. Its location provided a natural amphitheater for crowds to hear the speakers, and the property could accommodate more than 20,000 persons. It was also a safe location, protected from attacks by the Paterson police force. Haledon was a new, independent entity, and its mayor, a sympathetic German socialist named William Brueckman, was able to ensure the safety of workers. These Sunday rallies, often led by Hannah and IWW leaders, kept the strikers' spirits up and their resolve strong as their bellies became increasingly empty. With personal savings rapidly depleted, there was no money for rent, doctors, or druggists. A Relief Committee provided free medical and dental services, and many landlords understood the situation and did not evict strikers. But although the Purity Cooperative Company, founded in 1905 by immigrant Jews, offered free bread, hunger remained the biggest enemy of the strikers.

"We were out on strike six months," said Elizabeth Gurley Flynn. "I saw men go out in Paterson without shoes in the middle of winter and with bags on their feet. I went into a family . . . of eight children who didn't have a crust of bread, didn't have a bowl of milk for the baby in the house—but the father was out on the picket line. This was the difficulty that workers had to contend with in Paterson: hunger; hunger gnawing at their vitals; hunger tearing them down; and still they had the courage to fight it out for six months." We have no record of Hannah's feelings during this time, but we can be sure there were times she also was weak from hunger.

On the afternoon of June 7, Hannah, released from jail just in time, led 1,147 strikers from Turn Hall in Paterson through town to the railroad station and on to New York City. There they were joined by 800 more workers, and all marched from Christopher Street up Fifth Avenue, red banners flying and an IWW band playing "The Marseilles" and the "Internationale." Head high, Hannah led the procession, and her inspirational determination prompted Haywood to call her the "greatest little IWW woman in America."

The strikers were on their way to the most moving and brilliant spectacle of the entire walkout: the Paterson Strike Pageant. Conceived by writer/activist John Reed and supported by the New Intellectuals of Greenwich Village, who sympathized with the strikers' plight as well as the goals of the IWW, the purpose of the pageant was to publicize the strike and, most important, to raise money. With the backing of wealthy society matron Mabel Dodge and a host of left-leaning writers and artists, they were able to rent Madison Square Garden for one night. Reed trained more than 1,000 workers, including Hannah as a codirector, to reenact scenes from their strike as well as to sing songs from the IWW *Little Red Songbook.*

The letters "IWW" blazed 10 feet high from each side of the Madison Square Garden tower that night and could be seen from miles away. Fifteen thousand people, most of whom had walked from their homes, crowded the streets on every side of the gigantic building. The performance was delayed an hour while thousands found seats wherever they could. Many in the audience wept at the enactments of the funeral of a murdered striker, the portrayal of grinding millwork, the battles with police, the sending away of 700 starving children to foster homes, and the inspiring speeches and the songs sung. The next morning, newspapers that had either ignored or criticized the strikers wrote of the pageant as a great production and new form of art.

Soon after, Hannah led a group of fifteen Paterson strikers, girls aged fifteen to seventeen, on an overnight fund-raising trip to Coney Island. The girls wore white linen dresses, red sashes or scarves, and an IWW button. Each girl carried a small metal bank.

Despite rave reviews, an unforgettable production, and the further raising of political consciousness, the pageant failed miserably because it did not bring in the money the strikers so desperately needed. The expenses of the one-night performance were too high, the net proceeds only $1,996, and the audience too poor to make the hoped-for contributions. As a hostile press began accusing the pageant committee of lining their own pockets with monies earned, jealousy, suspicion, and dissension flared and marred the solidarity of earlier months. As the strike dragged on into July, sympathizers' funds dwindled, pickets were arrested more and more frequently, and despair and starvation took the place of determination.

The manufacturers had the greater advantage all along. They controlled the police and the courts. They controlled the media and "respectable" opinion. Mill owners could shift orders to their Pennsylvania plants, where there was plenty of cheap labor; 91 percent of the workers in the Pennsylvania silk mills were women and children. The Paterson strikers were literally starved back to work.

The dyers broke first under the pressure. The broad-silk weavers went next. On July 18 the ribbon weavers withdrew from the strike committee to begin negotiations with employers on a shop-by-shop basis. Their defection broke the IWW and the strikers. There would be no industry-wide settlement. Weak from hunger, spirits defeated, the strikers were forced to return to work under the same conditions they had left five months earlier. Although the silk industry in Paterson had been changed forever, it wasn't until 1919, mainly due to workers taking advantage of increased demand for silk and the low unemployment caused by World War I, that broad-silk and ribbon weavers won an eight-hour workday.

For some, like Hannah, times became even harder, especially without the exhilarating support of fellow strikers. Punished for being a leader during the strike, Hannah was blacklisted. It is not known how she spent the next nine years, although family members continued to work in the silk industry. In 1922 she married Harry Mandell, a thirty-nine-year-old Lithuanian Jew, and had two sons, Robert and Jack. Facing severe economic hardship during the Depression and after failing to make a living running a candy store in Brooklyn, the family went on relief for several years. Eventually Hannah and Harry bought a store in Paterson, where both worked eighteen-hour days. Hannah never spoke of her role in the strike in front of her children. Indeed, her son Jack did not learn of his mother's strike activities until the 1980s. Still, Hannah often spoke of Haywood, Flynn, and the IWW to Harry and was a special supporter of her younger brother, a mill hand in Paterson who continued to speak out against the owners. Hannah remained proud of her Jewish heritage but was not religious. The rest of her life was quiet and uneventful.

Getting immigrant or first-generation Jewish women such as Hannah to participate in strikes and to join labor organizations presented little problem to organizers, but keeping women active in union affairs was another matter. Hannah may have led marches when single, have been transformed and politicized in the course of the struggle, have gained a new visibility in the community, but once married she was no doubt pressured by habitual societal strictures to replace world concerns with concerns about household, husband, and children. In addition, sensitive to criticism that wages and conditions declined when women went into the factories, Hannah may have stepped back to let the men have the jobs. Surely she was aware of socialist rhetoric of such organizations as the IWW claiming that after the revolution women would be able to return to their happy homes and not have to work for wages. Doubtless, no one ever asked Hannah what she wanted to do. And so, she became merely a historical footnote.

It must have been difficult to go from outspoken leader to voiceless housewife. Hannah, however, was silent on this. She died on July 17, 1960, from a heart attack and is buried in King Solomon's Cemetery in Clifton. She is remembered in *Paterson* by P. G. Goodman:

> Annie Silverman, noble maid
> Led thousands of pickets on parade.
> Like Joan of ancient France,
> She led her troops around the plants.
> Rows of pickets in close formation,
> Till the Chief of Police blocks the demonstration
> Of pickets marching with even tread,
> And Annie Silverman at the head.

BIBLIOGRAPHY

Past & Promise: Lives of New Jersey Women. The Women's Project of New Jersey Inc. Meruchen, NJ: The Scarecrow Press, Inc., 1990.

MARY LUDWIG HAYS MACAULEY

Cunningham, John T. *New Jersey: A Mirror on America.* Florham Park, NJ: Afton Publishing Co., 1878.

———. *New Jersey: America's Main Road.* Garden City, NY: Doubleday & Company, Inc., 1966.

Downey, Fairfax. "The Girls Behind the Guns," *American Heritage: The Magazine of History,* vol. 8, no. 1 (1956): 46–48.

Ferling, John. *Setting the World Ablaze: Washington, Adams, Jefferson, and the American Revolution.* New York: Oxford University Press, 2000.

Gilman, C. Malcolm B. "Molly Pitcher—Mary Ludwig: The Huguenot Heroine of the American Revolutionary War," *The National Huguenot Society Proceeding,* vol. 16 (1959): 97–101.

Horner, William. *This Old Monmouth of Ours.* Freehold, New Jersey, 1932.

Karnoutsos, Carmele Ascolese. *New Jersey Women: A History of Their Status, Roles, and Images.* Trenton, NJ: New Jersey Historical Commission, Department of State, 1997.

Landis, John B., Esq. *A Short History of Molly Pitcher: The Heroine of the Battle of Monmouth.* Carlisle, PA: The Cornman Printing Co., 1905.

Landis, John B., Captain. "Investigation into American Tradition of Woman Known as 'Molly Pitcher,'" *The Journal of American History,* vol. 5, no. 1 (1911): 83–96.

Malone, Dumas, ed. *Dictionary of American Biography,* vol. 6, 574–5. New York: Charles Scribner's and Sons, (1935).

Massey, Gregory D. *John Laruens and the American Revolution.* Columbia, SC: University of South Carolina Press, 2000.

Norton, Mary Beth. *Liberty's Daughters.* New York: Cornell University Press, 1996.

Scholastic Encyclopedia of Women in the United States, 18. Produced by Sheila Keenan. New York: Scholastic, Inc. 1996.

Smith, Samuel Stelle. *A Molly Pitcher Chronology.* Monmouth Beach, NJ: Philip Freneau Press, 1972.

Stevenson, Augusta. *Molly Pitcher: Girl Patriot.* New York: The Bobbs-Merrill Company, Inc., 1960.

Thompson, D. W. & Schaumann, Merri Lou. "Goodbye, Molly Pitcher." *Cumberland County History,* vol. 6, no. 1 (Summer 1989): 3–26.

Vertical files of the New Jersey Historical Society.

Internet Sites

"American Women and the Military." US Military Web site: www.gender gap.com/military/Usmil1.htm.

"Camp Followers in the American Revolution." Historic Valley Forge Web site: users.erols.com/grippo/Campfollower.htm.

"18th Century Medicine-Care and Treatment of Battlefield Injuries" by Steve Cobb. 18th Century Medicine Web site: www.i-is.com/st.clair flats/wpmedicine3. htm.

"Historians Still Debate Molly Pitcher Story" by Susan Lindt. Sentinel Country Cumberland County Web site: www.cumberlink.com/50_in _250/pitcher_molly.html.

"Palatine History" by Lorine McGinnis Schulze. The Olive Tree Genealogy Web site: www.rootsweb.com/~ote/palatine.htm.

"Revolutionary War Weapons" by Tim Morley. Revolutionary War Weapons Web site: www.greeceny.com/arm/welch/weapons.htm.

SYLVIA DUBOIS

Berthold, Michael C. "'The Peals of Her Terrific Language': The Control of Representation in Silvia Dubois, a Biografy of the Slav Who Whipt Her Mistres and Gand Her Fredom," *MELUS,* vol. 20, no. 2. Los Angeles (Summer 1995).

Cunningham, Barbara, ed. *The New Jersey Ethnic Experience.* Union City: Wm. H. Wise & Co., 1977.

Gaspar, David Barry & Hine, Darlene Clark, eds. *More Than Chattel: Black Women and Slavery in the Americas.* Bloomington and Indianapolis: Indiana University Press, 1996.

Genovese, Eugene D. *Roll, Jordan, Roll: The World the Slaves Made.* New York: Pantheon Books, a Division of Random House, 1974.

Greene, Larry A., Harris, Leonard & Price, Clement A. "New Jersey Afro-Americans: From Colonial Times to the Present," *The New Jersey Ethnic Experience,* 64–87. Edited by Barbara Cunningham. Union City: William H. Wise & Co., 1977.

Hine, Darlene Clark, ed. *Black Women in America: An Historical Encyclopedia,* vols. 1 and 2. Brooklyn: Carlson Publishing Company, 1993.

Hodges, Graham Russell. *Slavery and Freedom in the Rural North: African Americans in Monmouth County, New Jersey, 1665–1865.* Madison, WI: Madison House, 1997.

Larison, C. W. M.D. *Sylvia Dubois: A Biography of The Slav Who Whipt Her Mistres and Gand Her Fredom.* Edited with a translation and introduction by Jared C. Lobdell. New York: Oxford University Press, 1988.

Loewenberg, Bert James & Bogin, Ruth, eds. *Black Women in Nineteenth-Century American Life: Their Words, Their Thoughts, Their Feelings.* University Park, PA: The Pennsylvania State University Press, 1976.

Morton, Patricia, ed. *Discovering the Women in Slavery: Emancipating Perspectives on the American Past.* Athens and London: The University of Georgia Press, 1996.

Stockton, Frank R. *Stories of New Jersey.* New Brunswick, NJ: Rutgers University Press, 1987, 1961.

ABIGAIL GOODWIN

Bacon, Margaret Hope. *Mothers of Feminism: The Story of Quaker Women in America.* San Francisco: Harper & Row, 1986.

———. *Valiant Friend: The Life of Lucretia Mott.* New York: Walker and Company, 1980.

Brown, Elisabeth Potts & Stuard, Susan Mosher, eds. *Witnesses for Change: Quaker Women Over Three Centuries.* New Brunswick and London: Rutgers University Press, 1989.

"Disgraceful," *Freeman's Banner* (June 28, 1837).

Farner, Thomas P. *New Jersey in History: Fighting to Be Heard.* Harvey Cedars, NJ: Down the Shore Publishing, 1996.

Greene, Larry A., Harris, Leonard & Price, Clement A. (Lee Hagan, coordinator). "New Jersey Afro-Americans: From Colonial Times to the Present," in *The New Jersey Ethnic Experience,* 64–87. Edited by Barbara Cunningham. Union City, NJ: William H. Wise & Co., 1977.

Harper, Robert W. "Abigail Goodwin: Abolitionist," *The Way It Used to Be.* Salem County Cultural & Heritage Commission, 1975.

———. "Runaway Slaves Found Refuge in Salem County," *Today's Sunbeam* (April 30, 1987): C1, C7.

———."South Jersey's Angel to Runaway Slaves." *Sunday Press* (June 15, 1975): 4–5.

Hodges, Graham Russell. *Slavery and Freedom in the Rural North: African Americans in Monmouth County, New Jersey, 1665–1865.* Madison, WI: Madison House, 1997.

Levin, Jay. "A Secret Path to Freedom," *New Jersey Monthly* (December 2000).

New Jersey Anthology. Compiled and edited by Maxine N. Lurie. Newark, NJ: New Jersey Historical Society, 1994.

Shourds, Thomas. *History and Genealogy of Fenwick's Colony.* Bridgeton, NJ: George F. Nixon, 1876.

Still, William. *The Underground Railroad.* New York: Arno Press and the *New York Times,* 1968.

Stockton, Frank R. *Stories of New Jersey.* New Brunswick, NJ: Rutgers University Press, 1987, 1961.

Wright, Giles R. *Afro-Americans in New Jersey: A Short History.* Trenton, NJ: New Jersey Historical Commission, Department of State, 1988.

Yellin, Jean Fagan. *Women & Sisters: The Antislavery Feminists in American Culture.* New Haven and London: The Yale University Press, 1989.

Internet Sites

African-American Mosaic: "Abolition." A discussion of abolitionist literature and songs from newspapers, periodicals, sermons, speeches, abolitionist society reports, broadsides, and memoirs of former slaves. Abolition Web site: www.loc.gov/exhibits/african/abol.html.

History and Geography of the Underground Railroad. Underground Railroad Web site: www.afgen.com/underground_railroad.html.

"Quakers of 19th Century Reform" by J. William Frost. PBS: Not for Ourselves Alone Web site: www.pbs.org/stantonanthony/resources/quakers.html.

"The 1783 Quaker Petition to Congress Regarding the Abolition of Slavery." Rootsweb Web site: www.rootsweb.com/~quakers/petition.htm.

LILLY MARTIN SPENCER

Bolton-Smith, Robin & Treuttner, William H. *Lilly Martin Spencer 1822–1902: The Joys of Sentiment.* Washington, D.C.: Smithsonian Institution Press, 1973.

Canaday, John. "The Resurrection of Lilly Martin Spencer," *New York Times* (July 29, 1973).

Edwards, Lee M. *Domestic Bliss: Family Life in American Painting 1840–1910.* Yonkers, New York: The Hudson River Museum, 1986.

Gerdts Jr., William. *Painting and Sculpture in New Jersey.* Princeton, NJ: D. Van Nostrand Company, Inc., 1964.

Greer, Germaine. *The Obstacle Race: The Fortunes of Women Painters and Their Work.* New York: Farrar Straus Giroux, 1979.

"Lilly Martin Spencer's Art Exhibited at Wellesley College," *Boston Sunday Globe* (November 4, 1973): A–38.

Montclair Art Museum Library. Clippings files on Lilly Martin Spencer.

Petersen, Karen & Wilson, J. J. *Women Artists: Recognition and Reappraisal from the Early Middle Ages to the Twentieth Century.* New York: Harper Colophon, 1976.

Rubinstein, Charlotte Streifer. *American Women Artists: From Early Indian Times to the Present.* Avon, 1982.

Schumer, Ann Byrd. "Aspects of Lilly Martin Spencer's Career in Newark, New Jersey," *New Jersey Historical Society Proceedings,* vol. 77, no. 4 (October 1959): 244–255.

Taylor, Robert. "Lilly Martin Spencer 1822–1902," *American Art Notes* (Winter 1984).

ANTOINETTE BROWN BLACKWELL

Blackwell, Antoinette Brown. *The Sexes throughout Nature.* New York: G. P. Putnam's Sons, 1875.

Cazden, Elizabeth. *Antoinette Brown Blackwell: A Biography.* Old Westbury, NY: The Feminist Press, 1983.

"Death Sounds Call For Mrs. Blackwell," *Newark Evening News* (November 5, 1921): 4.

Johnson, The Reverend Tony. "Antoinette Brown Blackwell: A Pioneer of Liberal Religion in New Jersey." Sermon brief—First Unitarian Church of Essex County, May 11, 1997.

Lasser, Carol & Merrill, Marlene Deahl, eds. *Friends & Sisters: Letters Between Lucy Stone and Antoinette Brown Blackwell 1846–1893.* Urbana and Chicago: University of Illinois Press, 1987.

Rossi, Alice S., ed. *The Feminist Papers: From Adams to de Beauvoir.* Boston: Northeastern University Press, 1988, 1973.

Internet Sites

"Distinguished Women of Past and Present." Distinguished Women Web site: www.distinguishedwomen.com/biographies/black-al.html.

National Women's Hall of Fame Web site: www.greatwomen.org/profile. php?id=19.

"NJ Women's History." Rutgers Web site: www.scc.rutgers.edu/njwomen shistory?Period_4/womenvoters.com.

"Western New York Suffragists." Winning the Vote Web site: www.winning thevote.org/ABBlackwell.html.

"The Birthplace of Hans Brinker" from *Stories of New Jersey* by the Federal Writers' Project of the Works Progress Administration (December 1936).

Clarke, William Fayal. "In Memory of Mary Mapes Dodge," *St. Nicholas* (October 1905).

Dodge, Mary Mapes, conductor. *St. Nicholas: An Illustrated Magazine For Young Folks,* vol. 16, part 1. New York: The Century Co., November 1888–April 1889.

———. *Hans Brinker, or the Silver Skates.* Philadelphia: George W. Jacobs and Company, 1924.

Hagerty, Alice. "James Mapes Dodge, Class of 1869—Noted Inventor, Industrialist, Humanitarian," *The Newark Academy Alumnus* (Fall 1985).

"Mary Mapes Dodge Dead," obituary in the *Tribune,* New York (August 22, 1905).

"Mary Mapes Dodge Dead," obituary in the *Sun,* New York (August 22, 1905).

"Mary Mapes Dodge Dead," obituary in the *New York Times* (August 22, 1905).

"Mrs. Dodge of St. Nicholas Dead," obituary in the *Herald* (August 22, 1905).

Roggenbuck, Mary June. *St. Nicholas Magazine: A Study of the Impact and Historical Influence of the Editorship of Mary Mapes Dodge.* The University of Michigan (dissertation): 1976.

Wilkonson Collection of Mary Mapes Dodge clipping files. Manuscripts Division, Department of Rare Books and Special Collections, Princeton University Library, Princeton, NJ.

Wright, Catharine Morris. *Lady of the Silver Skates: The Life and Correspondence of Mary Mapes Dodge 1830–1905.* Jamestown, RI: Clingstone Press, 1979.

Internet Sites

"Children's Periodicals in the United States During the Nineteenth Century and the Influence of Mary Mapes Dodge" by Erica E. Weiss. Mary Mapes Dodge, St. Nicholas Web site: www.facstaff.bucknell.edu/gcarr/19cUSWW/MMD/weiss.html.

"A Tribute to St. Nicholas: A Magazine for Young Folks" by J. L. Young. Flying Dreams Web site: www.mindspring.com/~jlyoung/nick.htm.

CLARA MAASS

Carlisle, Robert D. B. *Building Bridges for 125 Years.* Belleville, NJ: Clara Maass Health System, Inc., 1993

Clara Louise Maass: A Tradition of Caring. Belleville, NJ: The Clara Maass Foundation.

Cunningham, John T. *Clara Maass: A Nurse, A Hospital, A Spirit.* Belleville, NJ, 1968.

Guinther, Leopoldine. "A Nurse Among the Heroes of the Yellow-Fever Conquest," *The American Journal of Nursing,* vol. 32, no. 2 (February 1932): 173–176.

Internet Sites

"Clara Maass History." Clara Maass Medical Center Web site: www.saint barnabus.com/hospitals/clara_maass/history/index.html.

"Yellow Fever." Electronic Library Web site.

"Yellow Fever and the Reed Commission." University of Virginia Web site: www.med.virginia.edu/hs-library/historical/yelfev/par1.html.

JESSIE REDMON FAUSET

Davis, Thadious M. Foreword to the 1989 edition of *There Is Confusion* by Jessie Redmon Fauset. Boston: Northeastern University Press, 1989.

"Jessie Fauset: Midwife to the Harlem Renaissance," *The New Crisis,* vol. 107, no. 4 (July/August 2000): 24–25.

Kellogg, Charles Flint. *NAACP: A History of the National Association for the Advancement of Colored People, Volume 1909–1920.* Baltimore: The Johns Hopkins Press, 1967.

McDowell, Deborah E. "Jessie Fauset, 1882–1961," *Modern American Women Writers,* 123–139. Elaine Showalter, consulting editor, and Lea Baechler and A. Walton Litz, general editors. New York: Charles Scribner's Sons, 1991.

McLendon, Jacquelyn Y. *The Politics of Color in the Fiction of Jessie Fauset and Nella Larsen.* Charlottsville, Virginia: University Press of Virginia, 1995.

Miller, Nina. "Femininity, Publicity and the Class Division of Cultural Labor: Jessie Redmon Fauset's *There Is Confusion,"African American Review,* vol. 30, no. 2 (Summer 1996): 205.

Napier, Winston, ed. *African American Literary Theory.* New York: New York University Press, 2000.

Overton, Dr. Betty J. "Women Writers of the Harlem Renaissance: A Woman's Vision," *Themes in the Black American Experience: A Learning Literacy Program,* Dr. Jessie Carney Smith, Project Director. Fisk University Library, 1981.

Pryse, Marjorie & Spillers, Hortense J., eds. *Conjuring: Black Women, Fiction and Literary Tradition.* Bloomington: Indiana University Press, 1985.

Sato, Hiroko. "Under the Harlem Shadow: A Study of Jessie Fauset and Nella Larsen," *The Harlem Renaissance Remembered,* essays edited with a memoir by Arna Bontemps. New York: Dodd, Mead & Company, 1972.

Sylvander, Carolyn Wedin. *Jessie Redmon Fauset, Black American Writer.* Troy, NY: The Whitston Publishing Company, 1981.

Wall, Cheryl A. "Jessie Redmon Fauset, 1882–1961" in *Past and Promise.*

———. *Women of the Harlem Renaissance.* Bloomington & Indianapolis: Indiana University Press, 1995.

Watson, Steven. *The Harlem Renaissance: Hub of African-American Culture, 1920–1930.* New York: Pantheon Books, 1995.

Wilkinson, Brenda. *African American Women Writers.* New York: John Wiley & Sons, Inc., 2000.

Wright, Elizabeth, Kauffman, Bill & Beito, David. "Alternative Afrocentrisms: Three Paths Not Taken Yet," *The American Enterprise,* vol. 6, no. 5, 55.

ALICE STOKES PAUL

Faber, Doris. *Petticoat Politics: How American Women Won the Right to Vote.* New York: Lothrop, Lee & Shepard Co., Inc., 1967.

Flexner, Eleanor. *Century of Struggle: The Women's Rights Movement in the United States.* Cambridge: The Belknap Press of Harvard University Press, 1959.

Hirsch, Marianne & Keller, Evelyn Fox, eds. *Conflicts in Feminism.* New York and London: Routledge, 1991.

Irwin, Inez Haynes. *The Story of Alice Paul and the National Women's Party.* Fairfax, VA: Denlinger's Publishers, Ltd., 1977.

Kerber, Linda K. & De Hart, Jane Sherron. *Women's America: Refocusing the Past.* New York: Oxford University Press, 1991.

Kraditor, Aileen S. *The Ideas of the Woman Suffrage Movement, 1880–1920.* New York: Columbia University Press, 1965.

Lynn, Naomi B., ed. *Women, Politics and the Constitution.* New York and London: Harrington Park Press, 1990.

Mayo, Edith P. *Women in Politics: A History of American Women in Their Struggle for Equality.* Edited by Constance Minkin, Office of Exhibits Central. Circulated by the Women's Program, Smithsonian Institution for Women's Week at the Smithsonian Institution, October 3–October 7, 1977.

McGoldrick, Neale & Crocco, Margaret. *Reclaiming Lost Ground: The Struggle for Women Suffrage in New Jersey.* Produced in cooperation with the Women's Project of New Jersey, Inc. and the Drew University–Madison School District "Curriculum as Window and Mirror" series. Publication made possible by a grant from the New Jersey Committee for the Humanities, 1993.

Rosenberg, Rosalind. *Divided Lives: American Women in the Twentieth Century.* New York: Hill and Wang, 1992.

Stevens, Doris. *Jailed for Freedom: The Story of the Militant American Suffragist Movement.* New York: Schocken Books, 1976.

Tickner, Lisa. *The Spectacle of Women: Imagery of the Suffrage Campaign 1907–1914.* Chicago: The University of Chicago Press, 1988.

Internet Sites

"Alice Paul's Fight for Suffrage." The American Experience/Way Back: Stand Up for Your Rights Web site: www.pbs.org/wgbh/amex/kids/civilrights/features_suffrage.

"How Did the National Woman's Party Address the Issue of the Enfranchisement of Black Women, 1919–1924?" Original editorial project by Jill Dias, State University of New York at Binghamton, May 1997. Binghamton Women's History Web site: www.womhist.binghamton.edu/nwp/introduc.htm.

"Legendary Feminist: Alice Paul" by Sonia Pressman Fuentes. Moondance Web site: www.moondance.org/1998/winter98/nonfiction/alice.

"Paulsdale: Birthplace and Home of Alice Paul." Alice Paul Web site: www.alicepaul.org/paulsdal.

"Suffrage." Black Women and Suffrage Web site: www.rci.rutgers.edu/~elk/suffrageblackwomen.html.

"The Quiet of a Spinning Top: Alice Paul and the Women's Movement at Swarthmore" by Alisa Giardinelli. Swarthmore Web site: www.swarthmore.edu/bulletin/currentissue/paul.

"The War, Civil Disobedience, and the Nineteenth Amendment." Votes for Women Web site: www.huntington.org/vfw/stb/stb10.

ALICE HUYLER RAMSEY

"AAA Celebrates 100 Years of Service," *AAA Traveler,* vol. 35, no. 2 (March/April 2002): 1, 3.

Brown, Don. *Alice Ramsey's Grand Adventure.* Boston: Houghton Mifflin Company, 1997.

Brown, Don & Rochman, Evan. "Queen of the Road," *Biography,* vol. 1, no. 2 (February 1997): 48.

Evertz, Mary. "Woman Driver Makes History Then—and Now," *St. Petersburg Times* Online (October 20, 2000).

Georgano, Nick. *The American Automobile: A Centenary 1893–1993.* New York: Smithmark, 1992.

Holmstrom, David. "On the Road with Alice," *American History*, vol. 29, no. 3 (July/August 1994): 44.

Hyatt, Patricia Rusch. *Coast to Coast with Alice.* Minneapolis: Carolrhoda Books, Inc., 1995.

Ingraham, Joseph C. "From Hell Gate to Golden Gate—in 1909," the *New York Times*, section 12 (June 7, 1959): 53.

James, Louise Boyd. "From Coast to Coast" *Cobblestone* (July 1987).

Jensen, Cheryl. "By Blazing Coast-to-Coast Trail, She Helped Put a Nation on the Road," the *New York Times*, section 12 (June 6, 1999): 1.

Jensen, Cheryl and Christopher. "Following Alice," *Car & Driver*, vol. 45, no. 10 (April 2000): 113–117.

Kuralt, Charles. *On the Road With Charles Kuralt.* New York: G. P. Putnam's Sons, 1985.

Ramsey, Alice Huyler. "Veil, Duster, and Tire Iron," *Vassar Quarterly*, vol. 47, no. 5 (June 1962): 8–11.

———. *Veil, Duster and Tire Iron.* Covina, California, 1961.

Russell, Thomas H. *Automobile Driving Self-Taught: An Exhaustive Treatise on the Operation, Management, and Care of Motor Cars.* Chicago: The Charles C. Thompson Co., 1909.

Scharff, Virginia. *Taking the Wheel: Women and the Coming of the Motor Age.* New York: The Free Press, 1991.

Wiel, Georgette. "Drive! She Said," *Vassar Quarterly*, vol. 77, no. 4 (Fall 1981).

MARIA JERITZA

Armstrong, William. *The Romantic World of Music.* New York: E. P. Dutton & Company, 1922.

Branigan, Alan. "Jeritza Keeps Diva Glow in Her Newark Retirement," the *Sunday Star-Ledger* (May 26, 1974).

———. "Maria Jeritza: Front Row Center," *Newark Sunday News* (May 19, 1963): 6–8.

————. "Opera's Golden Age Lives in Memory of a Star Among Stars," the *Sunday Star-Ledger* (June 3, 1979).

Briggs, John. *Requiem for a Yellow Brick Brewery: A History of the Metropolitan Opera.* Boston: Little, Brown and Company, 1969.

Christiansen, Rupert. *Prima Donna: A History.* New York: Viking, 1985.

Decsey, Ernst. *Maria Jeritza.* Vienna: J. Fischer-Verlag, 1931.

Dizikes, John. *Opera in America: A Cultural History.* New Haven: Yale University Press, 1993.

Finck, Henry T. *My Adventures in the Golden Age of Music.* New York: Funk & Wagnalls Company, 1926.

Jeritza, Maria (translated by Frederick H. Martens). *Sunlight and Song: A Singer's Life.* New York: D. Appleton and Company, 1924.

Kolodin, Irving. *The Story of the Metropolitan Opera 1883–1950.* New York: Alfred A. Knopf, 1953.

Mayner, Harriet Anderson. "Maria Jeritza, 1887–1982," *Past and Promise: Lives of New Jersey Women.* The Women's Project of New Jersey Inc. Metuchen, NJ: The Scarecrow Press, Inc., 1990.

"Met Opera Star Cited," in *Newark News* (October 16, 1967).

Performing Arts Research Library at The New York Public Library, Lincoln Center. Scrapbook of Clippings and Programs, October 1921– November 1923.

Redmond, Michael. "A Final Bouquet to a Superstar of a Nobler Era," the *Sunday Star-Ledger* (July 18, 1982): 14.

————. "Newark Celebrating the 100th Birthday of an Operatic Legend," the *Sunday Star-Ledger* (August 23, 1987): 15.

————. "Newark 'Showcase' Shows off Grandeur in Yule Celebration," the *Star-Ledger* (December 13, 1983): 57.

Redmond, Michael & Shannon, Anthony F. "Maria Jeritza is Dead at 94, Newark Star of Opera World," the *Sunday Star-Ledger* (July 11, 1982): 1, 32.

Rockwell, John. "Maria Jeritza, Star of Opera's 'Golden Age,' Dies at 94," the *New York Times* (July 11, 1982): 24.

————. "Song by Richard Strauss Discovered," the *New York Times* (September 15, 1984): 11.

HANNAH SILVERMAN

Dodyk, Delight W. & Golin, Steve. *The Paterson Silk Strike of 1913: Primary Materials for the Study of the History of Immigrants, Women and Labor.* Via grants of The Garden State Immigration History Consortium and the New Jersey Department of Higher Education, 1987.

"'Fierce Every Way': The Paterson Silk Mills (1913)," from *Words That Make New Jersey History,* Howard L. Green ed. New Brunswick, NJ, 1995, 191–193.

"Find Editor Guilty in Paterson Trial," the *New York Times* (June 4, 1913): 1–2.

Flynn, Elizabeth Gurley. *The Rebel Girl: An Autobiography My First Life (1906–1926).* New York International Publishers, 1955, 1973.

Glenn, Susan A. *Daughters of the Shtetl: Life and Labor in the Immigrant Generation.* Ithaca and London: Cornell University Press, 1990.

Green, Martin. *New York 1913: The Armory Show and the Paterson Strike Pageant.* New York: Charles Scribner's and Sons, 1927.

Golin, Steve. *The Fragile Bridge: Paterson Silk Strike,* 1913. Philadelphia: Temple University Press, 1988.

Herbst, John. *Slice of the Earth.* Pamphlet produced by The American Labor Museum, Haledon, New Jersey, 1982. First appeared as an article in *New Jersey History* (99, vols. 1 and 2), the New Jersey Historical Society.

Karnoutos, Carmela Ascolese. *New Jersey Women: A History of Their Status, Roles and Images.* Trenton, New Jersey: New Jersey Historical Commission, Department of State, 1997.

Kornbluh, Joyce L., ed. *Rebel Voices: An IWW Anthology.* Chicago: Charles H. Kerr Publishing Company, 1988.

Norwood, Christopher. *About Paterson: The Making and Unmaking of an American City.* New York Saturday Review Press/E. P. Dutton & Co., Inc., 1974.

"Pickets' Ways Told to a Paterson Jury," the *New York Times* (June 5, 1913): 20.

Scranton, Philip B., ed. *Silk City: Studies on the Paterson Silk Industry, 1860–1940.* Newark, NJ: New Jersey Historical Society, 1985.

Songs of the Workers to Fan the Flames of Discontent, 33rd edition. Chicago: Industrial Workers of the World, 1970.

Tax, Meredith. *The Rising of the Women: Feminist Solidarity and Class Conflict, 1880–1917.* New York and London: Monthly Review Press, 1980.

Tripp, Anne Huber. *The I.W.W. and the Paterson Silk Strike of 1913.* Urbana and Chicago: University of Illinois Press, 1987.

Voices from the Paterson Silk Mills. Compiled by Jane Wallerstein. Charleston: Arcadia Publishing, 2000.

Weinberg, Sydney Stahl. *The World of Our Mothers: The Lives of Jewish Immigrant Women.* Chapel Hill and London: The University of North Carolina Press, 1988.

INDEX

ABOUT THE AUTHORS

Lynn Wenzel and Carol J. Binkowski co-authored *I Hear America Singing: A Nostalgic Tour of Popular Sheet Music* (Crown/Random House) in 1989 and are delighted to have worked together again on this project.

Lynn Wenzel's articles, essays, and reviews have appeared in *Newsweek*, the *New York Times*, *Newsday*, and *Ms.*, among many others. She was a contributing writer to the anthology *Past and Promise: Lives of New Jersey Women* and is a nationally syndicated feature writer on antiques and collectibles for such publications as *Antique Review*, *Antique Week*, *American Country Collectibles*, and *Victorian Design and Living*. She was managing editor of *New Directions for Women*, a national and international feminist newsmagazine, for many years. A California native, Lynn lives in the historic Sierra Nevada gold rush town of Nevada City, California, and shares her now-empty nest with her husband, Jeff.

Carol J. Binkowski is the author of *Musical New York: An Informal Guide to Its History and Legends & A Walking Tour of Its Sites and Landmarks* as well as articles that have appeared in *Clavier*, *The New York Daily News*, *The Optimist*, *The Instrumentalist*, and other publications. She is a reviewer for *Library Journal*. A pianist as well as a staff organist at the Church Center for the United Nations, she has presented performances and lectures throughout the New Jersey Public Library system as well as at such historic landmarks as South Street Seaport in New York City. A New York native, Carol lives in Bloomfield, New Jersey, with her husband, Richard, and daughter, Daria.

JUL   2003